EMPERORS
OF ADLAND

EMPERORS OF ADLAND

Inside the Advertising Revolution

NANCY MILLMAN

WARNER BOOKS

A Warner Communications Company

The passage from *Marion Harper: An Unauthorized Biography* is reprinted by permission from Crain Books, a division of National Textbook Company, 4255 West Touhy Avenue, Lincolnwood, Illinois 60646.

Book Design by Nick Mazzella

Warner Books, Inc., 666 Fifth Avenue, New York, NY 10103

W A Warner Communications Company

Printed in the United States of America
First printing July 1988
10 9 8 7 6 5 4 3 2 1

LIBRARY OF CONGRESS
Library of Congress Cataloging-in-Publication Data

Millman, Nancy.
    Emperors of adland : inside the advertising revolution / Nancy Millman.
      p.   cm.
    Includes index.
    1. Advertising agencies—United States. 2. Advertising—United States. I. Title.
HF6182.U5M56   1988
338.7′616591′0973—dc19   87-37190
                                             CIP

    ISBN 0-446-51403-9

FOR J.C.M.

ACKNOWLEDGMENTS

In the beginning of 1986 my job of writing a daily column about advertising and marketing for the Chicago *Sun-Times* changed dramatically. The kind of breaking news I began to cover shifted from new consumer products and trendy advertising campaigns to an essential restructuring of the industry itself.

Mergers and acquisitions became the hottest topic of the day, mirroring what was happening in the business world at large.

I am grateful to my readers, both the person-on-the-street and the advertising executive, who wrote to me and called during that time, to let me know that my coverage helped them understand the revolution in adland.

Leah Rosen, a former colleague at *Advertising Age* who was Chicago bureau chief of *People* magazine in the summer of 1986, stopped me on Michigan Avenue and told me I should expand the megamerger stories into a book. Her insistent suggestion was the true catalyst for this project.

For providing a foundation of knowledge and understanding, I owe a debt to my editors at *Advertising Age*, where I began working in 1976. Larry Edwards, who was Chicago bureau chief when I was a new reporter, was exceedingly generous in sharing his erudition and insight. As assistant managing editor and managing editor, Edwards gave me assignments that encouraged me to grow and he was always

ACKNOWLEDGMENTS

available to help me refine my ideas or tell me where to go for the facts.

Some of Edwards' bigger assignments led me to the tutelage of Joe Winski, the talented writer and editor-at-large. I am very grateful to Winski for teaching me about reporting, providing an example of excellence and encouraging me to do my best.

Larry Doherty, deputy editor of *Advertising Age*, has been most cooperative during the writing of the book, as well.

I'm also grateful to Robert Page, owner and publisher of the Chicago *Sun-Times*, for his role in making this book come about. Page undertook a major promotional campaign for my marketing column in 1986, and the visibility of those advertisements, notably in the *New York Times*, brought me to the attention of my agent Faith Hornby.

Faith's motherly support provided just what this first-time author needed to get her through all of the difficult periods of an extremely busy year.

The content of this book is a result of many interviews and a lot of research. Many of the people who helped me with facts, clarification, details, and introductions to other sources, prefer to remain unidentified. I am grateful for their trust and their contributions.

And the many executives who took time from their hectic schedules to share their insights on the record, thank-you as well.

Denise O'Neal, the skilled librarian at *Advertising Age*, devoted many of her weekends to putting together complete files on the companies covered in the book. Her excellent job is much appreciated.

I also am indebted to Sally Saville Hodge, former business editor at the *Sun-Times*, for her support during this project. She granted me the days away from the office I needed for research and the flexible schedule to enable me to write both a column and this book.

At Warner Books, executive editor Jim Frost and associate editor Charles Conrad were always cheerful, helpful and kind.

To my friends who were still there after I barely spoke to them for a year—thank-you.

And to my husband Jeff, whose enthusiasm, confidence, encouragement, and patience never wavered, I'll always be grateful.

—Nancy Millman

EMPERORS
OF ADLAND

"When I attempt to tell others about the current state of the ad agency business, it reminds me of nothing so much as Alice attempting to explain her presence in Wonderland: 'I can't explain myself, I'm afraid, sir,' said Alice, 'because I'm not myself, you see.'

". . . Certainly, the agency business is having difficulty explaining itself because it is not itself, at least not in a way that anyone in the business for more than a couple of years would recognize.

"We have altered not only the nature of the agency business, so that for the first time we are perceived, unhappily, as just another business . . . but the structure of the business as well.

"Because of it, the agency business has been stripped, perhaps permanently, of that special mystique it enjoyed. A mystique which made it different, and more than just another business."

—Charles D. Peebler Jr.
Chief executive officer
Bozell, Jacobs, Kenyon & Eckhardt
in a speech to the Magazine Publishers Association
American Society of Magazine Editors convention,
October, 1987

CHAPTER 1

It was an exceptional night for the party yacht *Liberty*. Robert Jacoby, chairman of the Ted Bates advertising agency, had invited the company's major shareholders and some of his special friends for a sunset sail on the rented boat to celebrate their newfound fortunes. When the yacht, which cost $10,000 for the night's charter, embarked from the Twenty-third Street pier on the East River, there were nearly one hundred millionaires on board.

Five days before, on August 7, 1986, the 320 Bates stockholders had received their payouts for the sale of the privately held agency Ted Bates Worldwide to a British company called Saatchi & Saatchi. The sale price was $507 million, $57 million higher than what Saatchi & Saatchi had told the London financial community and the press. But even at the publicly stated price of $450 million, it was the biggest deal in the history of the advertising business, a deal that left executives at other ad agencies gasping in disbelief.

Bates, an ad agency with a reputation for some of the most artless and offensive commercials on the air but with perenially high profits, had grown to be the third largest in the world, with $3.1 billion in billings and 5,000 employees.

The acquisition of Ted Bates by Saatchi & Saatchi was the

British firm's most dramatic move. It was sparked by the announcement, just weeks before, on Sunday, April 27, that BBDO International, Doyle Dane Bernbach, and Needham Harper Worldwide were uniting in the first three-way merger in the industry to create the world's biggest advertising firm, with $5 billion in billings. Two weeks later, when Saatchi made public its intention to gobble up Bates, the rankings were rewritten. Saatchi & Saatchi said it was climbing to the top, with billings of $7.5 billion.

Among the revelers on the yacht that hot August night was Ralph Rydholm, the roly-poly creative chief of the agency who had joined Bates from J. Walter Thompson Co. in Chicago only eleven weeks before the announcement of the sale. Rydholm, in his late forties, had spent most of his career at Thompson and had held the number-two spot in the Chicago office. But a management succession plan at JWT brought in an outsider instead of giving him the top Chicago spot, and Rydholm jumped ship.

Known for his ability to pen a catchy tune and link it with an appealing advertising idea, Rydholm had risked his creative reputation in moving to the Bates ad factory. But Jacoby knew he couldn't sell an agency that didn't have a topnotch creative chief, and he was willing to pay Rydholm a salary and bonus package of $400,000. That Jacoby was getting ready to sell the agency was no secret, and Rydholm knew that the lump sum he had to pay for Bates shares offered to him as an executive vice-president would quickly be converted into a handsome profit.

Wrinkling his puckish face into a squinty smile, Rydholm told a group of friends near the bar that his $1.4-million take represented "the highest hourly wage in the business."

As John Hoyne circulated through the crowd that night, he realized he had much to celebrate. The party represented the end of eighteen tiring months of shuttle diplomacy for the president of the Bates international division. For it was Hoyne, 47, who had been the chief dealmaker in the on-again, off-again merger negotiations in New York and London between his boss, Bob Jacoby, and Maurice Saatchi, now the co-owner of the world's biggest advertising conglomerate.

Hoyne wasn't much of an adman. He spent little time with Bates clients in his globetrottings to the agency's 102 offices. He took scant interest in the problems of the branches that reported to him, focusing instead on their profit obligations. And his colleagues said, rather jealously, perhaps, that he never spent more than two days in a row in the New York headquarters.

Hoyne is smooth and polished where Jacoby is tough and crass. His travels have given him an air of casual European elegance in his style of dress. Trim, with closely cropped gray hair and sparkling blue eyes, Hoyne was the most attractive man on the yacht.

Sharing with Jacoby the goal of maximizing the value of the company's shares, Hoyne had served as an effective buffer between the sophisticated British suitors and his brash boss. For his trouble, Hoyne reaped a personal profit of $17 million from the sale of his stock.

A chubby, bald executive who made $28 million in the Bates sale was not at all happy about boarding the *Liberty* that night. His presence was the result of a direct order from Jacoby, whom, after having been a friend and close associate for decades, he had come to despise. Donald Zuckert, a 52-year-old lawyer, had spent twenty-seven years as an account man at Bates and was now president of the company's flagship office in New York. Even in the boardroom Zuckert had a conversational style that could cross the borderline from colorful to crude, but his sharp intelligence and cultivated tastes in fine food and wines enabled him to hold his own with establishment clients.

Zuckert joked with his troops as the boat cruised New York harbor toward the Statue of Liberty, but inside he was seething with anger. It had been up to him to hold the agency together during the past year, as Jacoby and Hoyne neglected clients' business and internal concerns, concentrating instead on getting top dollar for the company.

And since the beginning of May, when the deal was announced, Zuckert's world had been rocked by the defection of many of the agency's biggest clients, including the company that had been with Bates since it opened its doors in 1940, Warner-Lambert.

But the past week had been especially trying for Zuckert. Unrest in the New York office, which had been building through the summer as more accounts were lost, reached a fever pitch on the day before the payout. Word spread quickly through the staff that Jacoby, during the first week in August, had arranged with his bankers for stock loans for two women in the company who did not meet shareholder requirements.

These two women were secretaries in their early thirties, one who worked directly for Jacoby and the other a very attractive and flirtatious brunette, whom the chairman considered to be his special friend.

Other shareholders, including Jacoby himself, had been struggling for years to make interest payments on their giant stock loans in order to be in a position to profit from the healthy escalation in the share price when they left the company or in case of a sale.

The two secretaries, on the other hand, were able to double their money overnight, having to pay only one day's interest thanks to their friendship with the chairman and his connections with the bank.

When news of Jacoby's generosity made its way through the agency, deserving employees who had been lobbying over periods of five to ten years for the opportunity to buy stock were outraged, and Zuckert was the one who had to listen to their complaints.

But Jacoby was oblivious to the controversy, and as host of the soirée, he was radiant. Strolling the deck during the outbound trip, with the younger of the two secretaries, Jennifer Van Liew, at his side, Jacoby looked like a man on top of the world. At age 58, Jacoby had accomplished his goal of becoming the country's richest adman. After years of schmoozing with clients and currying favor with his bosses, the diminutive CEO pocketed a personal take of $112 million in cash from the sale of Ted Bates. As part of the deal, Jacoby had signed a five-year personal service contract with Saatchi & Saatchi that would pay him $1.2 million in salary, bonus, and perquisites a year.

Jacoby cared little for the personal trappings of success. When he crossed his leg at the knee, his soft leather loafer often showed a hole in the sole. His suits, cut to fit his skinny 5'4" frame, were undistinguished in design, and his ties dated back to another decade. He wore the same tie bars in the eighties that had been in his jewelry box in the fifties, and his shirt collars were ill-fitting below the wattle of flesh that hung from his jaw.

But there are two accessories with which Jacoby is always identified. One is the big cigar that he nervously twirls and lights up at any hour of the day. The other is a small nickel-plated pistol that he keeps under his suit coat.

The yacht neared the Statue of Liberty, and Jacoby's attendant and driver, Ron Orr, brought him another Canadian Club and soda. A pair of executives on their way to the bar passed the center cabin and noticed a group of women seated around a coffee table. Jennifer Van Liew, Jacoby's personal secretary Eileen Drgon, and two older women employees of the agency—all rumored to have been very close to Jacoby during the past fifteen years—were engaged in friendly conversation. "I wonder what stories they're sharing," one of the new millionaires said, snickering to his friend.

Monica Jacoby, the charming and refined wife of the chairman, wasn't on the *Liberty* that August night. She had stopped attending these fetes, or any agency activities for that matter, years before. The mother of four daughters and now a grandmother, she preferred the quiet life at the couple's sprawling ranch house in America's most affluent suburb, Saddle River, New Jersey.

Monica was a devout Catholic, and her husband's notorious drinking and womanizing escapades probably had embarrassed her once too often.

During the past few months, however, Monica Jacoby was forced to assume a more public persona as part of another of her husband's activities. On May 14, just days after the sale of Bates was announced, Jacoby had been named chairman of the American Association of Advertising Agencies.

It was an honorary post that had been held by many of the eminent names in the industry, including Marion Harper, the founder of the Interpublic Group of Companies; Ray Rubicam of Young & Rubicam; Fairfax Cone of Foote, Cone & Belding; and Jacoby's predecessor, Archibald McG. Foster of Ted Bates. At the annual convention at the Greenbrier resort in the West Virginia mountains that spring, Monica had graciously appeared at her husband's side, fielding congratulations as the chieftains of competing agencies whispered about the "indecent" profit the Jacobys had reaped from the Bates sale.

The cruise was nearing an end, and Jacoby settled into a deck chair with Jennifer close at hand. His tipsy associates passed by the self-satisfied chief to bid him good night.

Not a single person on board the *Liberty* that night had any idea that it would turn out to be Jacoby's last public outing in New York. What Maurice and Charles Saatchi would learn in the next month about the man who finessed them into paying $507 million for a huge, but mediocre, ad agency would propel the advertising business back to the "huckster" image it had had in days gone by.

CHAPTER 2

Francisco Franco, the dictator of Spain, was the person to whom Bob Jacoby was compared by the executives who served him. He ruled the agency by intimidation and fear, using the promise of financial gain and the threat of financial punishment to manipulate his underlings.

Under Jacoby, it was money, rather than advertising, that was the driving force behind Ted Bates Worldwide. When he took over as chief executive officer in April 1973, the company was a New York ad agency with billings of $160 million. Jacoby, a Phi Beta Kappa economics graduate of Princeton University, made sure the agency was more profitable than any of its competitors by developing a strategy of growth by acquisition.

The agency was founded in 1940 by a former vice-president of Benton & Bowles, Ted Bates. His philosophy of advertising was based on a doctrine he called the Unique Selling Proposition—that each commercial message should offer an unusual benefit to the consumer. The concept of USP came to be well known in the advertising business through a book written by another Bates executive, Rosser Reeves.

Advertising slogans, including "Melts in your mouth—not in your hand" for M&M's and "Builds strong bodies 12 ways" for Continental Baking Co.'s Wonder Bread, came from the USP philosophy.

Other Bates brands, with the kind of advertising that many advertising professionals would have been embarrassed to see on the TV screen, included Preparation H and Certs. Products that catered to the mundane and the humiliating problems of the human condition. Hemorrhoids and bad breath.

The commercials were cheaply produced, had no pretentions to creativity, and hit the viewer over the head with the sales message. "Certs is a candy mint. No, Certs is a breath mint. Two. Two. Two mints in one."

The strategic thinking of the account managers at Ted Bates never caught up with the advertising of the 1960s and 1970s, when appealing to the heart became as important as appealing to the head. While firms such as Doyle Dane Bernbach and Wells, Rich, Greene were creating funny, emotionally appealing campaigns for Volkswagen and Benson & Hedges, Bates copywriters, under the stern direction of account men such as Jacoby, were hammering home the message that Anacin takes care of headaches "FAST, FAST, FAST."

Economics is not the run-of-the-mill background for an adman, but Jacoby turned it to his advantage. At Compton Advertising, the New York agency that had Procter & Gamble as its biggest account, Jacoby learned the ropes as a researcher and then as an account man, working on old-time brands from the household-products giant that makes Ivory soap and Tide detergent. Jacoby's specialty was Gleem toothpaste, advertised as the brand for people who "can't brush after every meal."

Cooking up ad strategies with the marketing boys in Cincinnati, selling the agency's creative executions to the conservative brand managers, and returning to his Fort Lee, New Jersey, home at two in the morning when it was time to plan the ad budgets for next year—all were part of Jacoby's training. And all "for about twelve grand a year" in the mid-1950s.

"I had nothing," Jacoby says. "My wife and I had four girls in five years, so I mean all we had was diaper money. I had to get in one day to Compton, it was payday. The night before, it was a snowy night, we were searching desperately through the house and getting all the old used Coca-Cola bottles so we could get the sixty cents or whatever I needed, so I could go in on the bus the next day and collect my paycheck from Compton. We were very close to the edge."

After joining Bates, and a brief foray to another agency to work on the Bristol-Myers account, Jacoby rose to the top based on his work on the chewing gum and candy brands sold by the American Chicle division of Warner-Lambert Co. Winning the favor of his clients and churning out exceptional profits from the Chicle business won him the favor of Archie Foster, then Bates chairman.

In 1969, Jacoby was named president of Bates, New York. He saw this job as his opportunity to take control of the company.

Jacoby says he worked eighteen-hour days during the week and twelve-to-fourteen-hour work days on the weekends. "Talk about guys who had no outside interests," says Don Zuckert, who worked for him. "His big joy on weekends was to go home and write memos—nasty memos." But his diligence pleased the agency chairman, and Jacoby got his break. Foster, the second man to hold the title of chairman of Ted Bates after the founder himself, took him aside and, as Jacoby tells it, said, "Bob, I'm getting out when I'm 60, and I'm gonna make you chairman and CEO and I'm going to give you the ownership shares."

"Those ownership shares, the controlling shares, the voting control shares, have passed from Ted, 100 percent of them, to Archie Foster, 100 percent of them, to me," Jacoby says. "And therefore what he did in essence was give me ownership of the agency. And that was a gift."

In contrast with other privately held agencies that helped to ease the burden on their shareholders by financing the giant stock payments through executive bonuses or loans from profit-sharing plans, Bates sent its shareholders to the bank to borrow the money.

"I'd been paying back a loan at Chase Manhattan Bank for 20 years up until [payoff day] when they finally got their dough back. Because I bought a lot of Bates shares, I went into hock up to my arse," Jacoby says.

While prestigious advertising firms such as Young & Rubicam and Ogilvy & Mather make their homes on Madison Avenue, Bates had its headquarters in 1515 Broadway, a sterile high-rise in the heart of seedy Times Square between Forty-fourth and Forty-fifth streets. Jacoby adored the building because of its bargain-basement rental price. In 1972, when the agency moved in, the rent was $6 per square foot, which more recently has climbed to $16, while other shops were paying in the neighborhood of $40.

Past the receptionist's desk on the twenty-seventh floor, the hallway leads to the executive offices. There were three oil portraits on the foyer wall: one of Ted Bates, one of Archie Foster, and one of Bob Jacoby. The painting of Jacoby showed the agency's third chairman with a huge cigar—a prop he is seldom without.

Members of the executive committee got used to the Macanudo smoke at morning meetings, but another of Jacoby's intimidation tactics was even more unsettling. In the safe in his office—a suite that had walls of windows overlooking the Hudson River—Jacoby kept a pistol. And during meetings he brought it out and placed it on the massive mahogany conference table just in case anyone forgot who was in charge.

Jacoby's overt gestures toward machismo, he admits, are attempts to make up for the greatest disappointment of his life. As a high school senior weighing 117 pounds, Jacoby won what he had aspired to most: an appointment to West Point. But standing barely 5'4", he says, he flunked the physical. He was too short.

When Jacoby took control of Bates, it was primarily a U.S. ad agency with a base of longtime major clients that, in addition to Mars Inc., Prudential, and Warner-Lambert, included Colgate-Palmolive, General Foods, American Cyanamid, and the U.S. Navy.

Jacoby perceived, earlier than most of his more statesmanlike competitors, that the way to a rapid rise in the ad-agency rankings was through acquisition.

"I saw that the way the world was going, there was going to be a conglomeration in the agency business. I figured at that time, and I was predicting to our guys in speeches, that there were going to be four, five, six big, big mega-agencies. I didn't coin the word, but in essence that's what I was describing.

"And I said we better be one of them, because we're gonna get middled otherwise. The ones in the middle, I said, are gonna be squeezed.

"And therefore we started saying hey, we gotta be working like crazy to get new accounts, but we're gonna have to buy some income. We're gonna have to buy."

Jacoby began to build a worldwide network, buying strong local agencies abroad and using them to service the company's multinational clients.

"He saw the company as having a single purpose," Zuckert said. "To support itself and to buy companies."

In the U.S., Jacoby bought midsized ad agencies much like his own—solid shops, often with creative reputations that were undistinguished—for which Bates could afford to pay top dollar. The strategy was to buy agencies in areas of the country where the advertising market was strong, with management already in place, so that the operational investment from Bates, in terms of time and money, was minimal.

Zuckert, the lawyer, was the man in charge of spotting and wooing the prey, and then negotiating the deals that promised the new subsidiaries autonomy.

Jacoby, meanwhile, "would kill to make sure profitability was such that the value of the stock increased by at least 20 percent each year," Zuckert says.

The Bates leaders before Jacoby had acquired two agencies —AC&R Advertising and Diener-Hauser in New York—as the first independent subsidiaries.

Stern Walters/Earle Ludgin in Chicago was the first deal negotiated by Zuckert in 1979. Another target was the Minneapolis-based agency Campbell-Mithun that had become successful because of its dealings with General Mills. Through the American Association of Advertising Agencies executive vice-president Harry Paster, an old-timer who knew everyone in the business, contact was established between Jacoby and the Campbell-Mithun principals, Stan Blunt and founder Ray Mithun. Mithun resisted the idea of a merger, championing the idea of a midwestern shop remaining independent. But the younger officers, seeing a chance to cash in early, and seduced by the profitability of the Bates stock they also would come to own, prevailed upon the old man. Zuckert conducted the negotiations with Ray Sachs, the agency's chief financial officer in Chicago, and closed the deal, boosting Bates farther ahead in the agency rankings.

Stern Walters/Earle Ludgin in Chicago, where Campbell-Mithun also had a branch, was next. Other units added along the way included Diener/Hauser/Bates, Conill Advertising, and direct marketing firm Kobs & Brady. An aging generation of executives looking to cash in made these deals possible.

Jacoby wasn't interested in interfering in the management of these regional shops. All he wanted was their profits.

"We'd just ship them numbers," says George Gruenwald, one of the officers of Campbell-Mithun who himself made a bundle on the sale to Bates. Gruenwald swears Jacoby never set foot in the Minneapolis office.

As Jacoby's dynasty grew domestically and internationally, the chairman's erratic behavior, often believed by his colleagues to have been brought on by too much alcohol, began to worry the board of directors. Jacoby made the international circuit his personal responsibility, taking eight trips to Europe and several to the agency's offices in the Far East each year. Monica Jacoby rarely accompanied him on these voyages, but often a young woman from the office, to whom Jacoby gave a title such as public relations manager, would travel with the boss, appearing on his arm at dinners with the local office executives.

Jacoby loved Australia and visited as often as possible. But while he was gone, on the other side of the world in New York Bates executives would arrive at their desks to find threatening telexes from their boss, sent in the middle of the night.

In the mid-1970s, while Jacoby was on a six-week trip to the Far East, some of the board members began to discuss openly their fears that the chairman's liquor consumption was stopping him from being objective about his behavior and was having a detrimental effect on the company.

Two groups of directors were formed, and one went to the agency's general counsel for advice, while the other group consulted the second-ranked attorney. The lawyers agreed that although Jacoby's behavior may have been objectionable, he owned controlling interest in the company and could dismiss the board if they offended him with a challenge.

Word of the consultations reached Jacoby as soon as he returned, and his interpretation of the events was that a cabal had tried to overthrow him. His retaliation was to force the corporate treasurer and general counsel, who between them owned 6,000 of the company's B shares, or voting shares, to sell their shares to him. The B shares carried fifty votes for every vote of A shares. Jacoby's version of the story is that he took over the shares when these two executives left the company. Nevertheless, then Jacoby owned all 30,000 voting shares, and his power base was absolute.

For a long period after this incident, Jacoby's public demeanor improved and his colleagues became less concerned about his drinking. "I had to drink to be successful in the advertising business," Jacoby was quoted as saying.

In February 1982, Bates made the biggest ad-agency acquisition that had taken place up until that time. William Esty Co., with billings of $450 million, became a Bates subsidiary for $55 million in cash.

The lucrative R. J. Reynolds tobacco business was what Jacoby was after. "You can take Salem out of the country, but you can't take the country out of Salem" was a well-known Esty theme for RJR cigarettes in the days when television and radio commercials for tobacco products made them the most profitable accounts. Now, instead of the profits going to the few distinguished executives who owned Esty, they would help to boost the value of Ted Bates stock.

The Esty deal, the first Bates had to finance through a long-term loan, helped to propel Bates into the biggest of the big-league agencies as far as billings were concerned. Bates could now boast that it was over the $2 billion mark.

What differentiated Ted Bates Worldwide from other agencies of the same size—Young & Rubicam and J. Walter Thompson Co., for example—was that the other giants had a guiding philosophy, a statement of purpose, a creative identity, that was communicated by their distinguished chairmen to employees around the world. Edward Ney, the chairman of Young & Rubicam, built an organization whose stated mission was to be the "best in the world at creating marketing and communications ideas which can help build a client's business." J. Walter Thompson, with Don Johnston at the top since 1974, may have had a fuddy-duddy creative reputation, but it was known as an agency of worldly gentlemen who catered to their clients' desires.

But aside from the dated Unique Selling Proposition, Bates had no philosophical foundation. On one of Jacoby's trips to Johannesburg, South Africa, he was being entertained by the local management at a dinner party in a restaurant. On his right was a young woman from the New York office who had accompanied him on the trip. Immediately after the dinner the telephone lines across the Bates network were buzzing with the chairman's philosophical declaration: "People ask me," Jacoby said, "what it takes to become a success in business. What's important to me is money, sex and revenge. If I don't get the first two, I'll get revenge on the person who kept them from me." Jacoby says he doesn't remember this statement. "But if I did say it," he explains, "I'd have a different order. I'd put revenge first, then money and sex."

Tales of Jacoby's international exploits became legendary, and they were perpetuated by the feisty chairman himself. On hotel stationery from around the globe, Jacoby would write notes to his managers about business concerns often peppered with descriptions of wee-hour revelries. The agency telex operator, the daughter of Jacoby's chauffeur, was occasionally the recipient of messages, with graphically obscene descriptions of his erotic encounters in distant lands.

And on the home front, Jacoby started spending fewer afternoons in the office and more around the corner in the comfortable masculine confines of Sardi's or in the back room of the dingy Footlights restaurant a few blocks away. The afternoon parties often included the agency's financial man, Don Murphy, and a secretary or two, who would return to the office "hanging on to the walls," in the words of one staffer on the executive floor.

No one would dispute that the sharp-minded Jacoby could

accomplish more between nine and noon than many executives could in an entire day. But his co-workers knew better than to schedule afternoon meetings—either he wouldn't show up or he would be so nasty the meeting would end in a ruckus. "If you saw him in the afternoon, he couldn't remember the next day what he had agreed to, or he'd deny he ever said it," one high-ranking Bates executive says, and others concur.

By early 1985, Jacoby was becoming frustrated. His desire to dominate a larger and larger share of the advertising market was being slowed by the difficulty of raising capital for his acquisitions. As a privately held agency, Bates had to go to the bank to borrow money for deals, while the publicly held shops, especially those traded on the London Stock Exchange, were able to raise capital simply by offering more shares on the market. He saw the specter of Bates slipping in the rankings, while the publicly held agencies leapfrogged ahead.

"Privately held," Bates told *Fortune* magazine in the summer of 1986, "Bates would be tenth next year and 15th the year after."

And now that he was in his late fifties, Jacoby wanted to make sure that he was going to get the best possible return on his Bates stock. Recycling the shares through the privately held shop—even the quickly climbing book value would have reaped the shareholders a tremendous profit—was becoming problematical.

"How do ya get rid of your shares?" Jacoby asked. "The young people don't want to put up the dough. They don't have the dough." Selling his empire to the highest bidder was Jacoby's solution.

On May 8, 1986, after a year and a half of discussions, Robert Jacoby and Maurice Saatchi signed the papers that would make the $3.1 billion Ted Bates Worldwide agency a subsidiary of Saatchi & Saatchi Co. PLC. Saatchi, in its announcement to the press, said it would now be "the world's largest advertising agency by a substantial margin, with billings of over $7.5 billion in 150 offices in 50 countries."

It was the biggest explosion in a series of quakes that profoundly shook everyone in the advertising industry, from corporate chiefs to copywriters. It would depose powerful executives, decimate strong companies, and create new empires.

Madison Avenue would never be the same.

CHAPTER 3

J eff Stark, one of the most talented copywriters at the London ad agency Saatchi & Saatchi, was ready to try something different in his career. His friend Dick Hedger had a small, successful agency and had been consistently wooing Stark to join him as a partner.

In the late 1970s Saatchi & Saatchi was the most talked-about shop on the tightly knit London ad scene. Charles and Maurice Saatchi, just barely into their thirties, were reeling in new accounts and winning creative awards faster than any of their competitors.

Stark is not a run-of-the-mill adman. He is a rumpled, casual man who has a real gift for humor, and he often takes his jokes onstage in London clubs to great response. An avid sailor and yacht aficionado, his primary ambition is to sail around the world.

After much deliberation, Stark chose the morning to tell his boss Tim Bell that he was resigning to join Hedger. Bell relayed the word to Charles, who was the agency's creative chief. "To hell with him," Saatchi said.

"But later in the day I presented a campaign to Charlie, and apparently he liked it a lot," Stark said. "So he handed me a piece of paper and told me to write down what it would take for me to stay at the agency.

"Well, of course, I doubled my salary, said I would not work on certain accounts, Procter & Gamble in particular, and asked for a guy as my art director. Just as a joke, I put at the bottom 'and a red Jag.' "

After taking a minute to make it clear that it pained him greatly to pay the price, Charles Saatchi said Stark could have it all.

The story has grown in London ad circles to include the coda that the next morning when Stark was leaving home to meet with Hedger and tell him he had been bought back by the Saatchis, a uniformed driver was waiting at the door with the keys to the Jag.

Charles Saatchi treats those he considers important to the company as members of his family. But apart from the inner circle, few Saatchi & Saatchi employees and even fewer people in the world outside the company have even met Charles face-to-face.

The U.S.-based senior vice-president in charge of public relations for Saatchi & Saatchi Compton, Janine Linden, was sent on a tour of the company's European offices.

A nervous New Yorker in her late thirties, Linden had the job of presenting the best image of the company to the press.

Over lunch in Rome, Linden brought up the mystery of Charles Saatchi to the creative director of the branch office in Italy.

"I've never met anyone who's seen him," Linden said to her host after several glasses of wine.

After lunch, Janine boarded the plane to London and, being a fearful flier, drank several more glasses of wine en route.

Upon landing in Heathrow, a representative from the London office met the plane and led her to a waiting car.

"Charles wants to see you," Linden was told. She protested that she didn't feel she was in the proper condition at the moment. "Right away," her escort added.

The car zipped into London, through the crowded streets, and across to 80 Charlotte Street on the edge of Soho. Pulling in behind the building, the car stopped next to Charles's Jaguar, which was parked alongside the trash bin.

Linden was ushered to the elevator and told to go to the sixth floor. The elevator ascended past the cramped and shabby offices that house the 750 writers, art directors, media buyers, and research and account staffers that made up Saatchi & Saatchi Compton, London, the company's flagship office.

As the elevator door opened, Charles was waiting. Wilted and filled with foreboding, Linden entered the private office.

"Sit down," Charles Saatchi said. "I heard you don't believe I exist. Well, I do. That will be all."

Charles Saatchi, who left school at the age of 18, began his career as a copywriter at Collett Dickenson Pearce, the leading creative agency in London. Two years later, in 1968, he started a creative consultancy with his art director—partner Ross Cramer. The idea was that Cramer Saatchi would be hired by London ad agencies for help in solving creative problems.

Charles Saatchi's writing brought controversy and attention to this little company. A poster for the United Kingdom's Family Planning Association is still cited as an example of the Saatchi style. The poster pictures a woebegone pregnant man and the headline "How would you feel if it were you who got pregnant?"

For the country's Health Council, the team produced a poster on the dangers of venereal disease. "Let's face it," the headline read. "You don't get V.D. from a lavatory seat."

Once his younger brother Maurice (in London, it's pronounced Morris) graduated from the London School of Economics, Charles and his partner broke up. The brothers, then 27 and 24, opened their ad agency called Saatchi & Saatchi & Co., with $1.2 million in billings.

Maurice and Charles Saatchi are the middle two of four sons born in London to a family headed by Nathan David Saatchi, a Sephardic Jew from Iraq who owned a textile business.

Today they each own shares worth more than $60 million in the largest marketing and communications services company in the world. In less than twenty years they have pushed Saatchi & Saatchi Co. PLC, the holding company for all of their subsidiaries, ahead of the oldest and best-established names in the advertising world.

They have taken the concept of a "full-service" advertising agency—an American idea of providing creative services, research, media buying, promotion, and direct marketing through one company—several steps further. According to Ron Leagas, a former managing director of the agency in London, "Saatchi has an absolutely unbounded, avaricious desire to be the biggest in everything they do. They don't see why they should be second best at anything."

By mounting the ad industry's most aggressive acquisition charge over the past decade, Saatchi & Saatchi has bought ad agencies, public relations firms, corporate communications companies, market research groups, and consulting companies.

This drive has led them to be dubbed "Snatch-it and Snatch-it," a moniker they are reported to find quite offensive.

J. Walter Thompson Co. was the first American ad agency to establish—in 1899—a London office as the base for its international expansion.

As JWT's international client base grew to include Ford Motor Co., Kellogg Co. of Battle Creek, Michigan, and the giant Unilever household products company, JWT dominated the London advertising scene.

The success of JWT paved the way for other American ad agencies to move in and to send out their tentacles to European, and eventually Asian, capitals on the strength of their relationships with multinational marketers. Companies such as Procter & Gamble, Coca-Cola, and Philip Morris enabled these agencies to build billings and revenues as they popularized their brand names in Europe, and the London offices of the U.S. shops were even becoming successful in poaching prestigious British companies, such as breweries and automakers, as their clients.

Despite the formidable and well-funded competition from America, Saatchi & Saatchi, by the end of 1979, less than a decade after opening with nine people, was the biggest agency in London. It surpassed all of the U.K. and U.S. agencies, including the venerable J. Walter Thompson Co.

The 1960s were the heyday of creativity in advertising in New York.

The brilliant William Bernbach and his gifted followers at Doyle Dane Bernbach were breaking new ground with advertising for Volkswagen, Avis, and Orbach's.

The zany bunch at Wells, Rich, Greene introduced a longer cigarette, Benson & Hedges, with humor that poked fun at both the product and the consumer.

A new breed of writers and art directors was bringing vitality and good taste to advertising, making it an art form in itself.

In London, the youngest and the brightest in the field were following this New York trend and giving it their own British twist.

Charles Saatchi was one of the creative superstars in London. But to Charles, creativity was not an end in itself. It was a positioning statement, a selling point, for the new Saatchi & Saatchi agency. From the day they began in 1970, with only Jaffa oranges, Granada Television, and the U.K. Health Council as their first accounts, Charles and Maurice set themselves apart with their audacity and ambition.

In the announcement of the formation of Saatchi & Saatchi, in the October 12, 1970, issue of the U.S. weekly trade paper *Advertising Age*, it was reported that "Saatchi & Saatchi is the first agency to throw aside completely the 15 percent commission system. With his brother, Charles Saatchi has evolved a method of payment which costs clients an average of 22 percent. He remarked, 'That makes us just about the most expensive agency in the business.' "

The arrogant brothers called the 22 percent a "performance fee which guarantees cheaper media buying as well as more effective work."

Maurice Saatchi said, "Gallup's research shows that print work has a terrifying low impact. The average reading score for a full-page ad in a national paper is 26 percent." The fledgling agency said it would guarantee that it would do better.

How could these two upstarts—Maurice, the subdued, gentlemanly, educated brother, and Charles, erratic, artistic, and aggressive—dare to tell the advertising world they were better than anyone else?

They were "immature as businessmen" when they began in 1970, says Leagas. But the Saatchis were "extremely dynamic and terrific opportunists . . . already they had great ambitions and a clear vision."

Maurice and Charles carefully cultivated the image of the company as a highly creative enterprise, but except for clients that Charles took a personal interest in, neither of them had much involvement with the advertising itself. These tasks were left to Tim Bell, often called "the third Saatchi," Ron Leagas, and creative director Jeremy Sinclair, all of whom were with the brothers from the beginning. Bell and Leagas now head competing companies.

Creating an image for the company was the domain of the brothers, as well as the planning strategies for growth.

"Charles has the ambition, and Maurice carries it out," Jeff Stark says.

Romancing and sometimes manipulating the gossipy London trade press was a key component in the Saatchi strategy. Maurice had developed important contacts in that field, having gotten his start in business as the promotions manager for *Campaign*, the popular weekly owned by the small Haymarket Publishing company.

"Charles would call me every week and tell me everything that was going on in town," says a *Campaign* reporter. "He knew who was moving where, what accounts were changing hands. And he'd let me know about every new campaign coming out of Saatchi's, and all of their new business."

Such cooperation produced a positive article about Saatchi & Saatchi on the front page of the influential *Campaign* practically every week. New ads were given glowing reviews, while account losses and business failures were minimized. The attention Saatchi was receiving was quite out of proportion to its size or importance in the ad community at that time.

Not content with the trade press, Charles even concocted publicity stunts for the London *Sunday Times*. He once called the business desk to warn them that he had insured his staff for $1.5 million against their being hired away.

Charles wanted all of his competitors to know about his acquisition ambitions years before they would begin to take him seriously. He wrote letters to rival agencies asking to buy them. But at that time, the dignified agency chiefs in London considered this behavior to be impertinent.

All of these antics were part of the strategy to position Saatchi & Saatchi. What Charles was trying to do for his company is the same thing his executives were promising to do for their clients. Create top-of-mind awareness for the Saatchi & Saatchi brand.

At the same time, the Saatchi brothers began to create an aura of mystery about themselves as individuals. The ongoing publicity effort focused solely on the company. Charles especially began to shroud himself in a veil of secrecy. His friends say he is quite shy. But his behavior ranges to the bizarre.

Once, one of the reporters Charles telephoned each week was at the Charlotte Street headquarters to visit another executive. As the elevator doors opened, a receptionist called out, "Hello, Charles." Although with his spiky hair and baggy black Japanese designer clothes the man only slightly resembled the few photographs she had seen, the reporter then realized that it was indeed Charles Saatchi riding the elevator with her.

"Charles," she said, introducing herself. "It's so nice to meet you after speaking with you on the phone all this time." He turned to face her, stuck out his tongue, and rushed off at the next floor.

The Saatchis separated themselves from the rest of the British advertising world by refusing to join the industry trade association. The group had an ethics policy that forbade stealing accounts from competitors. Early on, the brothers set up their system for wooing new business—a SWAT-team approach that pursued target companies relentlessly. That system has developed into a computerized science that is in place in all of the Saatchi & Saatchi offices around the world.

The brothers' strategy brought early results, and in the first few years the company grew to $10.5 million in billings, with new accounts such as British Leyland automobiles, Associated Newspapers, Bristol-Myers, and Dunlop tires.

Just as J. Walter Thompson Co., the paragon the Saatchis wanted so much to overtake, had expanded internationally with its automobile clients, so did the Saatchis journey into France, Belgium, and Holland with British Leyland as its lead client.

These ventures, begun in 1973, showed the Saatchis were serious about international expansion, but did not contribute much to the billings growth the Saatchis were seeking. The attempt to buy a French agency, Opta Dragon, ended before the deal closed, and a British shop, acquired during the same time, was written off as a loss shortly thereafter.

But the principal reason the brothers were stymied in their plan to soar to the top was that they failed to attract package-goods advertisers as clients—the category of advertising that makes the big shops really big. J. Walter Thompson, Young & Rubicam, Leo Burnett, Ogilvy & Mather—all grew because their biggest clients sold the most mundane products. Commercials for soaps and detergents, cereals and soups, candy and colas—the stuff of everyday life—are what paid for television programming and put money in the coffers of the giant ad agencies.

In 1975, the year that Bob Jacoby in Manhattan was cooking up his plans for growth, Maurice and Charles Saatchi in London were coming to the same conclusion.

If you can't win new accounts, you have to buy them.

CHAPTER 4

In the fall of 1975, Saatchi & Saatchi demonstrated it could change the rules of the ad game. But few were paying attention.

The Saatchi brothers, lusting after the package-goods brands that were taking their competitors into the billings big league, set their sights on the biggest player in this game: Procter & Gamble.

The number-one advertiser in the United States, Procter & Gamble also has broad-reaching international distribution and consequently is a large advertiser in the major European capitals. It was the biggest client of Garland-Compton, a publicly held ad agency in London.

Undaunting to the Saatchis was the fact that Garland-Compton, with billings of more than $40 million, was more than twice the size of the Saatchis' London agency. Financial savvy, always a stronghold of the Saatchi brothers, would give them the power in the company they sought to acquire.

Twenty percent–owned by Compton Advertising in New York, one of Procter & Gamble's most important U.S. agencies, Garland-Compton was the opposite of Saatchi & Saatchi in its approach to advertising.

The P&G method of advertising development, whether in

the U.S. or abroad, calls for carefully planned strategy and many kinds of testing of an advertising idea—focus groups to measure consumers' emotional responses and overnight recall tests to determine the communicative qualities of the copy, for example. Creativity is last on the agenda, and the advertising—up until the very recent past—shows it. Even in countries such as England and France, where wit and flair play a major part in the commercials on television, P&G spots are the typical slice of life. The housewife's dilemma over dirty laundry or the neighbor's recommendation for the best-tasting coffee. They often are little more than a translation into the local vernacular of the tried-and-true formula advertising that sells the product to housewives in America.

Besides P&G, Garland-Compton had Rowntree Mackintosh and United Biscuits as its biggest clients—just the kind of mainstream advertising that the Saatchis needed for growth.

Garland-Compton management, which had been seeking a merger partner, wanted to enhance its creative reputation. A union with the hot Saatchis was seen as a means to this end. So Saatchi & Saatchi sold itself to Garland-Compton in a stock and cash deal. But because Garland-Compton stock was widely held, and management owned an insignificant number of shares, the Saatchi brothers, with ninety-two percent ownership of their own private company, ended up with controlling interest in the merged agency. It was, in effect, a reverse takeover.

The Garland-Compton deal paid Saatchi four hundred thousand pounds, close to a thirty percent stake in the company, and gave it a New York base. And through this deal, the Saatchi brothers gained the ingredient that would be the key to their future: a listing of the London Stock Exchange. In 1977, the young executives restructured what they had bought into a new public company to enable them to take over even more control of the equity from "the Americans" who owned shares in the

New York Compton organization. The Saatchis then had a thirty-six percent stake in the company.

Saatchi & Saatchi Garland Compton, as the merged company was called, became the number-four ranked agency in the U.K. behind three U.S.-owned firms: J. Walter Thompson, Masius Wynne-Williams, and McCann-Erickson.

Charles and Maurice put their man Tim Bell in charge of running things while they sat on the board of the company, uninvolved for the most part in the clash of cultures that they had created with this deal.

Because of the difference in approaches between the two companies, the London ad community predicted doom for the Saatchi-Garland union.

But because any self-respecting ad person would rather create good ads than dull ones, and Tim Bell was a powerful and charismatic leader, it worked. In consort with Jeremy Sinclair, the creative director who had been with the Saatchis from the beginning, Bell operated successfully with the methods that had made the fledgling agency prosper.

Charles Saatchi, in addition to planning the overall strategy for the corporation, worked with Sinclair as creative director on important campaigns that especially interested him—accounts that the agency brought in from the creative consultancy, including the Health Education Council, and influential accounts that were to come.

The strength of the venture brought the confidence of clients, who jumped aboard.

Procter & Gamble awarded the agency major chunks of new business, including a big detergent brand called Ariel. British Leyland also moved in new business, as did Schweppes, with new drink brands.

As the company grew, so did the need for even more sophisticated financial management. The Saatchis recruited a 32-

year-old countryman with a Cambridge University degree and a Harvard MBA named Martin Sorrell. Sorrell, short, bespectacled, and hardworking, became the financial director and led the Saatchis to a new corporate structure.

The youthful holding company board members—Maurice, Charles, Sorrell, and David Perring—had specific tasks: Sorrell, the financial director, Charles, the strategist, Maurice, the public persona, and Perring, the corporate secretary.

Maurice set out on an intensive campaign to change the opinion of the City of London's financial community regarding advertising agency stocks—in particular, the company he controlled.

The volatility of the ad agency business—in which a company's fortunes could quickly sink if it was deserted by a major account—led analysts and investors to believe that the agencies were not a sound bet. Agencies have few assets, and the most important ones—talented people—could be easily lured to the latest hot shop with a quickly escalating salary or be dumped when a major account loss brought a drop in revenues.

As Saatchi & Saatchi Garland Compton grew, through acquisitions in Scotland, Ireland, and England, Martin Sorrell set up a financial reporting system that was unique in the advertising business and one that gave Maurice something to sell to the City.

The privately held companies the Saatchis acquired, unaccustomed to profit pressures and strict financial controls, found a whole new world awaiting them. The holding company took control of financial reporting for the entire company. The chief financial officer of each operating unit, formerly responsible for yearly and long-term financial forecasting, was now required to prepare monthly forecasts for the holding company management.

The holding company financial team made weekly and daily checks on the cash balances at each of the units in order to detect any problems at the unit before they became serious.

Saatchi & Saatchi group left the financial people in place at their acquisitions temporarily, but this heavyhanded management style usually led them to quit in frustration after a short time. Then the Saatchis could put their own bean counters in place to milk the profits from their acquisitions.

It was Margaret Thatcher, the Conservative Party candidate for prime minister of England in the spring of 1979, who really put Saatchi & Saatchi on the map.

Tim Bell and Ron Leagas, the actual managers of Saatchi & Saatchi Garland Compton, the flagship ad agency of the burgeoning holding company, were skeptical about the benefits of taking on the $4 million Tory party account in the fall of 1978. They worried about the effect that such a high profile account would have on their other clients. Would Procter & Gamble, on whom they so depended for growing revenues, feel neglected? And because of the uncertain outcome of the election, the admen feared the effect of negative publicity.

But the Saatchi brothers realized how the influence they could gain through helping Mrs. Thatcher to a Tory victory would shape their future. And they were right.

In this important effort, Charles Saatchi came down from his ivory tower and got involved in the creation, while agency chairman Bell, a flashy young man who drove a Ferrari, planned the strategy.

The Saatchi agency packaged Mrs. Thatcher like their clients package supermarket products. She was coiffed just so and dressed in suits and two-tone pumps. The promises she made in her campaign—to cut taxes and to bring new life to the economy— were just what the British people needed to hear.

The aggressive ad campaign began with a poster that charged the competing Labour Party with falling down on the job of curing unemployment. "Labour Isn't Working," read the headline over a long line of people heading toward an unemployment office. The word in London at the time was that the line for the photograph was made up of Saatchi staff members. Another poster in the same vein showed another line of people heading toward a hospital sign under the headline "Britain Isn't Getting Any Better."

The advertising throughout the campaign challenged the credibility of the Labour government and presented them as having been responsible for unemployment and industrial decline.

The Labour prime minister James Callaghan put off calling the election for the fall of 1978 until the spring. Conditions during the hard times of the winter helped give more credibility to the Saatchi-created campaign. Public opinion turned against the party in power.

The Saatchis' tactics were attacked by the Labour Party's Denis Healey, Chancellor of the Exchequer, who called the approach "rent-a-fake politics." Healey was reported to have said he found it unsurprising that Saatchi & Saatchi, who made its living promoting detergents and deodorants, should have been chosen to "cleanse and sweeten the image of extremism and division" created by Mrs. Thatcher.

But the Tories won the election. And Saatchi & Saatchi, given credit for revolutionizing political advertising in the U.K., took credit for having made Mrs. Thatcher.

Not only was the clear-cut marketing success of putting Mrs. Thatcher in No. 10 Downing Street evident to all of the country's businesspeople, but the new government's policies had many fans among business leaders.

In the summer following the May 3 election victory, the Saatchis saw their SWAT-team approach to new business come to fruition. After the first few years of relentlessly phoning potential clients at their competitors' shops, the Saatchi agency found that its newfound fame brought new accounts pouring in the door.

Here's how an article in the British magazine *Business* described the Saatchi new-business effort. "Despite their dynamic fronts, a lot of agencies are pretty laissez-faire organizations," the magazine quoted a former employee as saying. "Whenever Saatchi read in the press that a client was reviewing his account, the first reaction was: 'Right, who knows him? Get on the phone, now.' The second response was to kick the new business director in the balls for not getting us on the shortlist beforehand."

One of the biggest new business wins during that time was British Petroleum, which was reported to be worth $36 million in billings during the three-year period beginning late in 1979.

Nestlé and IBM also awarded pieces of their accounts to the Saatchi agency in London.

The Saatchis were moving into the same league with the top three agencies in the U.K., all of which were American-owned. By the end of 1979, J. Walter Thompson, McCann-Erickson, and D'Arcy MacManus & Masius all had about $145 million in billings. And based on its new business successes, Saatchi was getting close.

In 1979, another agency chief in London, the flamboyant Peter Marsh of Allen Brady & Marsh, was quoted as saying, "A year ago I had lunch with Maurice Saatchi. He told me that before too long Saatchi & Saatchi Garland Compton would be the biggest agency in Britain, that we would be No. 2, and that no one had yet awoke up to it."

Peter Marsh was not the only one getting that word from Maurice Saatchi.

The intelligent, polite, and charming brother dove into his corporate role enthusiastically, romancing the financial men of the City with the story that an aggressive creative agency like its flagship shop could also be very stable and profitable.

The company's 1979 results showed that Maurice was right. The company had "turnover" or billings of $153.7 million for all of its subsidiaries and posted a pretax profit of $5.3 million, up 30 percent. It was the company's ninth consecutive year of billings and profit growth.

Saatchi & Saatchi's profit margins of about 4 percent were way ahead of the industry average in Britain of 2.65 percent. The company had no debt and had lost virtually no accounts.

The company's share price on the London Stock Exchange boomed.

In the last quarter of 1979, Saatchi & Saatchi Garland Compton overtook J. Walter Thompson for the number-one spot in the London advertising billings race.

And the brothers turned their sights on America.

CHAPTER 5

Maurice Saatchi, having successfully wooed the London investment community and gaining plaudits for the company's financial performance in 1979, turned his charms on the men who headed the U.S. ad agencies.

"Many advertising people viewed Saatchi & Saatchi much like the blind men in the fable about an elephant," wrote John O'Toole, former chairman of Foote, Cone & Belding. "One man, feeling its trunk, decided an elephant resembles a snake; another, touching its leg, described the beast as being much like a tree; the third reached up, grasped its tail and pronounced it as a sort of rope.

"I probably would have formed my view in a similar way had it not been for a breakfast meeting at the Pierre Hotel one morning in the summer of 1981. It had been set up by a third party who called on me to determine whether I'd be willing to meet with Maurice Saatchi.

"As I drove down a virtually empty New England throughway that morning, visions of a glittering acquisition for Foote, Cone & Belding danced in my head. And as Maurice talked of his belief in pan-European and even global brands, as he admitted the necessity for his agency to break out of its London fetters and gain access to a worldwide network, I knew what Jimmy Carter meant by lusting in his heart.

"But all too quickly the conversation took an unexpected turn. It was halfway through the scrambled eggs that I began to realize what was going on: *Maurice wanted to buy FCB*. I have never, in the ensuing years, underestimated the dimensions of Saatchi & Saatchi's vision or its determination to realize it."

Few agency chairmen were denied the experience of a breakfast or a dinner with Maurice Saatchi. But before the Saatchis could actually make their move in the States, they needed two things: a stronger power base in the U.K. and a bigger stash of cash.

The Saatchi company's financial director Martin Sorrell devised a plan that would become the company's model for its acquisitions to come. Saatchi & Saatchi bought GDCH Holdings, a publicly traded company that owned Dorland Advertising, which was the eleventh biggest in the U.K.

Saatchi paid £5.6 million for Dorland. After the £1.5 million initial cash sum, further payments were to be parceled out in stages, with the profit performance of Dorland to determine the final amount.

Sorrell and the Saatchi brothers didn't like going to banks for a loan; they wanted to keep any debt off the company's balance sheet. To raise the funds for the Dorland deal, the company used "share placings" or "rights offerings."

Current shareholders were offered the right to buy a fixed number of new shares at a price that was about 15 to 20 percent below what the stock was trading at the time.

For the Dorland deal, £3 million was raised through the rights offering, and the rest would be paid through the company's cash reserves. Of course, because much of the sum to be paid was based on Dorland's future earnings, those earnings would in turn help Saatchi pay its debt to Dorland's owners.

* * *

The Dorland deal gave Saatchi & Saatchi two separate advertising agencies in London, and in their very carefully worded press statements, the Saatchis went to great lengths to stress the separateness, autonomy, and independence of the two companies. There was even to be competition between the two.

The idea was to have two strong ad agencies under the same ownership, which was not to interfere in their operation, thus convincing client companies who compete in the marketplace that it was permissible to place their accounts within the same family of ad agencies.

Saatchi & Saatchi did not originate this idea. It was appropriated from the Interpublic Group of Companies in New York and from the unusual man who was the pioneer of the mega-agency, Marion Harper. The story of the rise and fall of Marion Harper gave Maurice and Charles a case history to study before launching their own campaign for dominance of the advertising world.

Born in Oklahoma City in 1916, educated at Andover Academy and Yale, Harper was a marketing whiz who rose from office boy to president of the giant McCann-Erickson agency by the time he was 32. The son of a successful New York adman, Harper had a vision he developed on the way up. And from the day he was named head of McCann in 1948 he pursued it: to make his advertising operation the biggest in the world—the undisputed winner of the ad agency billings race.

J. Walter Thompson Co. was the target to beat, and in 1961 Harper made his first move in that direction.

In 1961 McCann-Erickson was a major international agency, with forty-six offices in sixteen countries, some of which were the biggest in their markets. McCann's key to international growth was the Atlanta-based Coca-Cola company.

Harper, an intense, balding man with heavy black glasses and a pointy chin, had six years earlier wrested the Coke business from the D'Arcy agency in St. Louis. By 1954, its U.S. market share was declining and the brand, known around the world, had stopped growing.

Harper and his associates developed a pitch to Coca-Cola management that positioned Coke as a global brand that needed a worldwide marketing strategy. Harper also pioneered for Coke the creation of an organization to serve Coke bottlers around the globe. McCann-Erickson already had a worldwide network in place, and to have Coca-Cola advertising handled through each of its international offices would guarantee their existence and profitability for years to come. Through this pitch McCann won the entire Coca-Cola account, worth $25 million in 1956, one of the biggest advertising budgets in the world.

Capturing a larger market share for his clients' products wasn't enough for Harper. He was driven to do the same in the advertising market for the agency he headed. But the bigger an agency got, the more it was blocked from new accounts because of the concept of conflicts with current clients.

A company with Coca-Cola, for example, which wages an expensive battle in the marketplace each day against other soft drink companies, would not tolerate any of its suppliers—for that is the context in which an ad agency is viewed—working in any way, anywhere in the world, for one of its competitors.

Perhaps the most stringent of any company in this regard was Procter & Gamble, which has long been the biggest spender of any advertiser in the world. As Procter & Gamble continued to march its American products into international markets, the assignment went to agencies who had no ties with competitors such as Unilever.

Loyalty to this concept was a way for ad agency management to prove its loyalty to their clients. And it was the clients who dictated what they did and did not consider to be conflicting accounts.

Harper's plan was to increase his company's share of the market by finding a way to circumvent the conflict problem.

Early in 1961, he established a holding company called Interpublic Inc., which was to be the parent company of McCann-Erickson and another agency called Marschalk & Pratt that McCann had acquired in 1954.

In February, Harper made advertising history by announcing that after a year of negotiations, he was acquiring a major British ad agency, Pritchard, Wood & Partners.

Interpublic purchased all of the stock of Pritchard, Wood, which had billings of $12.5 million, about the same as the McCann office in London.

"The arrangement means Interpublic will control eventually two international agency chains—McCann, which is American-run and American-based, and PWP, which will be British-run and British-based," chairman Sinclair Wood told the trade magazine *Advertising Age* during the announcement.

"This is the way the world is going," he said. "We've seen it happen in other business spheres, and advertising must go the same way."

Harper's Interpublic, instead of having to go out and compete for prestigious accounts, had bought them. With the PWP acquisition, the agency gained such clients as Rover cars, Cadbury, the giant candy company, Glaxo Laboratories, Britain's largest ethical drug manufacturer, and other major accounts.

During the next two years, Interpublic went about acquiring ad agencies and related companies around the globe. Harper's vision was not limited to agencies that did mainstream TV, radio, and print advertising.

He snapped up everything from a public relations firm in New Zealand to companies specializing in advertising measurement and communications research, merchandising and sales promotion—the full gamut of marketing communications.

By the autumn of 1963, Interpublic had grown to $413 million in billings. J. Walter Thompson Co., the largest U.S.-based ad agency, was reporting billings of about $420 million.

On a Sunday in October 1963, only twenty-four years after he started at McCann-Erickson as an office boy fresh out of Yale, Harper made a deal that boosted Interpublic ahead of world leader J. Walter Thompson. Borrowing heavily from New York banks to finance the deal, Harper paid an undisclosed cash sum to the management of another ad agency called Erwin Wasey, Ruthrauff & Ryan.

The new Interpublic subsidiary had billings of $83.5 million, and the advertising trade press, in apparent astonishment, called it the biggest agency deal in history.

Adding the billings and accounts of Erwin Wasey boosted Interpublic to very close to a half billion dollars in billings and into the number-one spot in the rankings.

Erwin Wasey had on its account roster Rolls-Royce automobiles, while McCann-Erickson handled the Buick division of General Motors. Both agencies did work for oil companies—Wynn Oil Co. in California was a client of Erwin Wasey, while McCann handed the Humble Oil account. And in a display of what was considered to be unusual arrogance, few clients of either agency were notified in advance that Erwin Wasey was to be sold. And if they were notified, their approval of the alliance was not considered to be an issue with the management of the agencies involved.

Interpublic took an aggressive stance on the conflict question—one that would be considered foolhardy today, and intolerable to clients.

Adding to the fact that most of the clients learned about the maneuverings in the newspapers rather than from their contacts at the agencies, Harper put out a statement that said Interpublic would "welcome an examination of the separateness of EWRR by any client or prospect, and will cooperate fully in answering questions. We are confident that actual experience will establish this separateness to the complete satisfaction of clients."

Harper's vision was praised in the press as paving the way for advertising agencies to become major companies—to allow them to grow in the same way that their clients were growing. An editorial in *Advertising Age* the week following Harper's ascension to the number-one spot compared his philosophy with that of marketing giant Procter & Gamble.

P&G is generally credited with having decided long ago that competition between brands was inevitable, and that no brand—not even the most impressive—could garner more than a share of any market. Therefore, said P&G, if we must split the market with other brands, why should they not be our own brands instead of some other company's?

Just as quickly as he bought his way to the top, Harper let his empire get out of control. The consummate marketing man, a stunning presence in client meetings, Harper nevertheless was a financial neophyte.

By 1965, Interpublic's organizational chart looked like a giant garden overgrown with weeds. The holding company controlled seven marketing services companies under the heading of Communications Affiliates and nine separate independent advertising agencies. The Interpublic Group, still a privately held company, had a staff of fifteen top executives, all highly paid and contributing to increasingly unmanagable overhead costs.

Harper himself, the largest single shareholder with 100,000 shares of Interpublic's 530,000 shares of class B stock, had a twenty-year contract commencing in 1965. The contract was to pay him $250,000 annually as of 1967—a sum that would increase each year—plus expenses and a share of profits.

Harper's dream was propelled by ever-increasing debt loads, and profitability did not keep pace. Though total billings of the Interpublic holding company increased, primarily through acquisition, the company had a net loss of $250,000 in 1966. The next year the company lost $4 million.

Just four years after reaching his goal of worldwide ad agency dominance, Harper had let his empire slip into financial ruin.

The company's cash reserves had slipped below the $10 million required by the banks, and in late 1967, Interpublic defaulted on a $2 million loan payment.

The authoritarian visionary had surrounded himself with layers of expensive talent who padded the payroll and isolated him from problems and feared disagreements. These top executives were beginning to realize that Harper's extravagant style was putting the company at risk. The bankers, who because of the degree of indebtedness of the company were in a position to approve or disapprove any major Interpublic act, voiced their alarm to the company's top echelon.

In 1967 the company's chief financial officer, Bill Taggart, learned from Interpublic's bankers that the company was technically in violation of its loan agreements. The banks had the right to demand full payment of the entire debt. Such a move would force Interpublic into receivership.

In October, the two banks requested a meeting with Interpublic board members, who included Carl Spielvogel, Bob Healy, and Taggart. Harper, whose spending style had caused the crisis, did not attend. The Interpublic team answered questions about client stability and media payments and talked about cost-cutting. Then one of the bankers mentioned the possibility of receivership. Although the boardmembers were able to avert the crisis by making it clear that the bankers would be in worse shape if they had to run the advertising business themselves, they knew the time had come to deal with the problem of Marion Harper.

Russ Johnston described the solution in *Marion Harper: An Unauthorized Biography*.

At precisely 10 o'clock, November 9, 1967, Harper rose and walked the short distance down the hall to the board room. The other directors were already assembled. A pot of tea with a Limoges cup and saucer were at the head of the table near Harper's oversize, blue leather chair.

One of the directors, seated on Harper's left, was Carl Spielvogel, whom Harper had hired from the *New York Times* to become PR director and who had achieved a spectacular rise for someone with no advertising-agency experience. Spielvogel had proved his value in many ways, including setting up contracts with major underwriting firms. If Interpublic ever got its house in order, he felt it was surefire for a public stock offering.

Taggart sat next to Spielvogel. He was a tough-talking, rough-looking but competent accountant. To his left was David Williams, 47 years old, handsome, slightly corpulent, well dressed. He was the second-largest stockholder, in the best position to challenge Harper's growth policy, but his faith in Harper was so strong he never had.

Across the table, secretary Don McNamara sat with his corporate records and notes quietly talking with Bob Healy, who was seated beside him. McNamara was the coolest member of the group, perhaps because of his legal training. Poised and proper at all times, he was the perfect model of a corporate attorney. No crisis, legal or otherwise, could ruffle him. Healy, as usual, was friendly, affable, and agreeable. A no-nonsense executive, he had the respect of all his associates and the agencies' working staffs.

Besides Harper, there were six people. All had been brought

into the company by him. All had been elevated to lofty, high-paying positions by him. All had shared his dream for the future. But not all had continued to approve of how he pursued that dream.

Harper smiled pleasantly at the group and opened the meeting. For almost twenty years he had conducted such meetings—first for McCann-Erickson, then for the other companies as they joined him one by one—not always as chairman, but always as the man with the power to make or break, hire or fire, approve or disapprove. There was no reason to suppose today would be different.

Harper started to read the first item on the agenda but was interrupted by one of the directors who requested permission to question Taggart about his latest discussions with the banks and to ask for a quick report on Interpublic's current financial situation. Harper saw no reason to deny permission, although the questioning was out of order on the agenda.

Taggart read swiftly from the current operating statement and reported that the financial situation had grown worse since the last board meeting. He recapped his conversations with the banks. Williams commented that if the figures were true, Interpublic was in violation of the loan agreements and asked Taggart if the banks could take over the company by forcing it into receivership. Taggart reluctantly said that was true.

There was silence. The electricity in the air was palpable. Then one of the directors spoke up.

Although these are not his actual words, in effect he said: It would seem that we are faced with a grave situation. None of us wants to see everything we have worked for go down the drain. The banks don't know the first thing about running an advertising agency. They would sell off the parts as fast as they could, and that would be the end of it. What we need is time to get hold of our business. As I understand it, the banks are not inclined to give us any more time as things stand. Therefore I move that the first order of business should be the replacement of our chief executive officer.

The motion was immediately seconded, and for the first time in his life, Marion Harper sensed danger. Then he relaxed. The motion was made by one of his strongest critics and seconded by another. There were four other votes around the table. In a move he undoubtedly would regret for the rest of his life, he put the motion to a vote. There were six votes in favor, none against.

Marion Harper rose and without a word left the room.

CHAPTER 6

It was a bloody battle that brought the Interpublic Group of Companies back to profitability and its eventual place among the giants of the industry.

Harper, 51 years old, deposed and disgraced, fought to retain his place by promising to help win new accounts. He told his colleagues he could bring Trans World Airlines into the Interpublic fold. But the debt-ridden Harper, who had borrowed heavily to finance his close to 20 percent stake in the company, did not succeed in his last personal campaign.

Harper personally owed Interpublic $800,000 and the banks more than $1 million. Though he lived in a lavish style—his pied-à-terre in New York was a suite in the Waldorf-Astoria—he was reported to have little more than it took to cover his living expenses.

The company bought back the stock and the board was glad to have the 100,000 shares available as a source of capital. But until the new chiefs of Interpublic were able to liberate the company from Harper's contract, worth at least $5 million, bankers were not interested in backing the company.

The eventual settlement with Harper cost Interpublic $2.5 million, and the high-living architect of the world's first mega-agency had to use most of it to pay his debts.

By February 1968, negotiations to end Harper's twenty-year contract were complete. Within weeks, Harper sold his English Tudor home in Westchester County, his three-plane charter airline company, and Interpublic's private jet. He sold his ranch and his cattle and disappeared from view.

The new corporate team headed by Robert Healy started slashing at the vast network established by Harper. Close to 1,000 people were cut from the company's payroll. The swiftness and depth of the staff cuts sent a giant shiver down Madison Avenue, as employees and managers of competitors watched what could happen when costs were allowed to soar out of control.

Consolidations among the myriad ad agencies and communications companies that had existed as independent entities became necessary. One of the extravagances of Harper's Interpublic empire was an independent company called Center for Advanced Practices, a creative think tank. In addition to its New York office, it occupied a twenty-five-room former inn, restored to opulence, in the Bavarian Alps. The center and other small units were folded or assimilated into the mainstream ad agencies as the new management team moved to cut overhead by $7 million.

The cutbacks brought the confidence of the financial community, and Chase Manhattan Bank stepped in with a revolving line of credit up to $10 million.

After the disaster of posting a close to $4 million loss for 1967, Interpublic's new management acted decisively to earn a profit of $3.6 million the next year. For 1969, profit rose to $4.8 million.

While the team at the top executing these controls was made up of executives close to retirement age—Robert Healy had been brought back from semiretirement in Florida at the time of Harper's ouster—one of the young stars to emerge from the morass was the short, red-headed Carl Spielvogel.

Spielvogel was right alongside Harper as Interpublic grew

and garnered a great deal of power in the organization, as well as a hefty salary for a former journalist. But on the day the board voted Harper out of the picture, Spielvogel's was one of the votes against his mentor. Because of his close association with Harper, many believed Spielvogel would not survive the purges of Healy and the new management team.

But instead of getting thrown overboard, Spielvogel became one of Healy's most trusted lieutenants, heading a group of small subsidiaries and remaining on the corporate board.

As a reward, in 1969, Spielvogel was named executive vice-president and general manager of McCann-Erickson, the largest agency in the Interpublic chain.

Spielvogel, moving from the corporate side to direct involvement in the ad agency business, would now be in a position to develop close relationships with clients. A soft-spoken gentleman, Spielvogel had a great deal of personal charm, and he very successfully forged linkups with the top marketing men and chief executives of important McCann client companies.

By the spring of 1970, the multidimensional Harper-style organization had disappeared, and the streamlined operation consisted of the following: McCann-Erickson, with billings of $511 million, and the third-largest agency in the world; Marschalk Co., with billings of $60 million; Erwin Wasey Inc., which had declined from the $79 million it billed when Harper bought it to $72 million in billings; Pritchard Wood, with $13 million in U.S. billings; and Jack Tinker & Partners, a $28 million agency.

After flirting with extinction under Harper, Interpublic thrived in the early 1970s, continuing to grow through acquisition and forging more of the biggest merger deals ever seen in the ad business.

One deal was sparked by the coveted jewel of the Chevrolet division of General Motors, a client of the privately held Detroit ad agency Campbell-Ewald. Interpublic, through its McCann-

Erickson subsidiary, was the primary ad agency for the giant U.S. automaker in countries outside of the United States. In addition to handling the Buick account in the U.S., McCann advertised the Opel, a General Motors car built in Germany, in all of its international markets.

Executives of Campbell-Ewald had been courted by "just about everybody," said chairman Thomas B. Adams.

Campbell-Ewald had held the Chevrolet account for fifty years, as the brand became the symbol of an "American car" and the media budgets multiplied through the early years of television. By 1972, Chevrolet cars and trucks were backed by $80 million in advertising spending, one of the single biggest budgets in America.

But Campbell-Ewald was, on the down side, totally dominated by the Chevrolet account. If Chevy were to decide to switch agencies for any reason, or to move part of the business to another shop for some fresh thinking, it would have been very destructive to the agency, whose total billings were $122 million. In November 1972, Interpublic agreed to pay the forty Campbell-Ewald shareholders the equivalent of $12 million in exchange for ownership of the agency. The linkup with Interpublic gave management insurance for the future, as well as considerable fortunes.

Adams, in talking about the deal, used the model of the organization of General Motors as a rationale for the sale of the agency, a tactic the advertising world would see repeated as merger mania spread into the 1980s.

"We seem to have been able to put together a microcosm of the General Motors pattern, where there are competitive divisions responsible to a central office, and if it does anything, it will probably increase or enhance competition among the various agency segments that make up Interpublic," Adams said.

Joining up with the giant Interpublic was similar to "what's happening to every other form of business, including automobiles, insurance, the grocery business, pharmaceutical, you name it—the smaller either had to disappear or join with others, and you have fewer and larger in order to be economically sound."

The deal put the Interpublic conglomerate very close to the $1 billion mark on the billings chart, way ahead of its nearest rival, JWT, which was in the $800 million range.

Working from a position of leadership, Interpublic prospered through the 1970s. McCann-Erickson, its biggest agency, brought to television some of the most popular commercials of the decade.

Coca-Cola, still McCann's biggest account, stayed on top of the soft drink market with heartwarming, upbeat musical commercials for Coke. "It's the real thing," viewers were told, in expensively, slickly produced spots that set the standard for big-budget advertising. Picking up on the spirit of youth that had calmed down from its protest days of the 1960s to a decade of love-thy-neighbor mellowness, McCann and Coke put hundreds of young people from around the globe on a scenic mountaintop to sell a soft drink with the message "I'd like to teach the world to sing in perfect harmony . . . I'd like to buy the world a Coke to keep it company."

Miller Brewing Co., a Milwaukee-based subsidiary of the giant Philip Morris tobacco company, was also making advertising history with a campaign for its Lite beer. Retired athletes such as Bubba Smith and other notables—Rodney Dangerfield and Micky Spillane, to name two—communicated that the new brew had all the taste of a great beer but was less filling. The good-humored campaign created a new category of beers and propelled Miller Lite to the top in record time.

Carl Spielvogel, the handpicked associate of Interpublic founder Marion Harper, had continued to climb in the holding-company hierarchy in the years following Harper's demise, and in the late 1970s he was vice chairman and chairman of the executive committee. He was in line for the top spot. But he lost out in a power struggle with tough-talking Philip H. Geier, who was tapped to succeed Paul Foley as chairman.

In May 1979, Spielvogel abruptly resigned from Interpublic. A few weeks later, William Backer, vice chairman and creative director of McCann-Erickson, the man who had developed the creative staff and was the final word on Coke, Miller, and all of the other commercials emanating from McCann, also resigned from his post.

Backer was a southern gentleman from Charleston, S.C., whose passion was horses and whose personal trademark was a bow tie. Spielvogel was a self-described "street-smart New Yorker." "We are not what you'd call bosom buddies," Spielvogel said.

But late in June 1979, the unlikely duo put out calls to the trade press to join them in a suite at the Gotham Hotel in Manhattan.

They announced the formation of a new ad agency. It appeared as if Backer and Spielvogel had been secretly planning their venture with clients and advertising associates, and their bombshell surprised and scared the New York ad community.

Two middle-aged pros they were, Backer at 53 and Spielvogel at 50, with decades of experience between them. Their contacts and personal friendships ran into the highest ranks of some of the most sought-after advertising clients in the country.

Spielvogel, the corporate executive, was to assume the same role in the new venture, and Backer, of course, would recruit and build a creative department and cast his discriminating eye and ear on all of the agency's work.

The former *New York Times* advertising columnist knew how to make good copy for readers. "We're not 25," Spielvogel said at the press conference. "We come out of the world's largest ad complex, and together stand unchallenged as the world's smallest agency."

Spielvogel carefully positioned the new agency as a maverick shop, intent on strong creative work. But he also set it apart with a kind of hard-boiled attitude that said, in effect, We are the best even though we're just starting out. "We're looking for the kind of client that knows the difference between good advertising and froth," Backer said.

Although they had financial backers but no apparent business at the time of their announcement, Spielvogel insisted on one point. "We're not interested in outside investors and won't ever go public."

The new agency executives, who had worked on some of the biggest ad accounts in the world, made it clear from the outset that they had no interest in the small, no-name accounts that the typical beginning shop attracts. To the regret of McCann-Erickson and Interpublic management, they did not have "no-compete" clauses in their employment contracts and were therefore free to poach as they liked.

It soon became obvious that Bill Backer and Carl Spielvogel may have lined up their team and their first client months before breaking away from the Interpublic fold.

"We were the ones doing all the work on Miller," one of the original six partners said. "So why should we do it for another company and not for ourselves?"

Within weeks of the announcement of the formation of Backer & Spielvogel, Miller Brewing Co. yanked its $85 million account—including High Life, Miller Lite, and Lowenbrau brands—from McCann-Erickson. And it landed at Backer & Spielvogel.

Accounts weren't all Backer & Spielvogel poached. The entire Miller team of account men and creatives became the original partners in the agency, splitting ownership and signing on for a six-year partnership.

Within a year Backer & Spielvogel was billing $100 million. Spielvogel's friendship with executives from Philip Morris, the parent company of Miller, also netted a new product assignment from another Philip Morris unit, Seven-Up Co. The soft drink expertise of Bill Backer had not succeeded in ripping Coca-Cola or any of its brands from the Interpublic family, but the introduction of caffeine-free Like cola from Seven-Up was a good place to start in the big-spending soft drink business. In a competition with New York's major-league heavy hitters, including Benton & Bowles, D'Arcy MacManus & Masius, and Wells, Rich, Greene, Backer & Spielvogel also won the account for the Liggett Group's Paddington Corp. brands, which included J&B Scotch.

And in that first year, Backer & Spielvogel was able to get its foot in the door at the Campbell Soup Co. with a special assignment. Eventually Backer was able to wrest from BBDO the mainline Campbell Soup business, putting Bill Backer's musical talent to work to introduce a campaign that would change the tide of prepared food advertising: "Bring on the Campbell's, Soup is good food."

Spielvogel was very vocal with his promises about the new shop. In interviews with the trade press, he set out his strategy, which eliminated international expansion except on the demand of a major client, and vowed that one agency principal would always be involved in each piece of business.

"And we want to remain private," Spielvogel stressed, noting the equity shared by only the six original partners. "Nothing is for sale here except our services," he insisted.

In an office that was occupied by Doyle Dane Bernbach in its heyday—at 20 W. 43rd St., it overlooked the New York Public Library—Backer & Spielvogel was the hot shop in New York.

CHAPTER 7

In the Chicago ad agency that made McDonald's Corporation advertising the lively, song-filled celebration of family and fun that it was in the late 1960s and 1970s, a bearded creative director was developing a loyal following. Keith Reinhard, the man who put his personal mark on all of the McDonald's work at Needham Harper and Steers, was being compared to the advertising greats of the preceding generation. His colleagues likened him to Leo Burnett of the giant Chicago agency that bore his name because of Reinhard's insight into advertising problems and his finely tuned creative approach. He had the ability to correctly set the mood and tone of an advertising campaign so that it perfectly reflected the image the company—such as General Mills or State Farm Insurance—was trying to communicate.

Reinhard also mirrored the great Burnett because of his total immersion in and dedication to his agency's work.

"Our mission," Reinhard would say, "is to create advertising that wins sales and wins praise. Anything that wins sales but abuses public sensibilities is shortsighted."

Reinhard, a deliberate man who speaks softly and slowly, was also compared to William Bernbach, the New York ad man who founded the most elite bastion of creativity in advertising,

Doyle Dane Bernbach. Like Bernbach, Reinhard inspired his people to do their best work.

He had a tremendous motivational effect on his co-workers. "In the words of the Budweiser Light commercial, Keith was always able to bring out your best," says Joel Hochberg, who succeeded him as the creative chief of the Chicago agency. "You're always somewhat afraid you'll forget to bring out your best. You're not afraid because you think he would holler at you, but because he'd be disappointed."

The world's number-one fast-food chain, McDonald's was the biggest client of Needham Harper and Steers, the ad agency where Reinhard grew up in the business. Reinhard was indispensable to McDonald's management in Oak Brook, Illinois, which paid for hundreds of commercials a year through the Needham operation. With billings in the '60s of about $10 million, McDonald's represented half of the revenue of the Chicago office. Reinhard developed a close friendship with McDonald's chairman, Fred Turner, and that clout put him in a powerful position for a young creative director at the agency.

Reinhard inspired almost cultlike fervor in the dedication of his colleagues to make McDonald's the premier advertising account in the country. Reinhard believed that through the visibility of the extravagantly produced and often poignantly written McDonald's commercials, Needham would become the premier creative ad agency in the country.

Reinhard's first job related to the world of advertising came in his early teens in his hometown of Berne, Indiana. He did odd jobs for a man who owned a popcorn wagon, and Reinhard bought it from him and painted it with the sign RINEY'S CORNER. His mother attached it to the family car, and they would drive around the village selling popcorn to bring in a little money to the household.

Berne is a Mennonite community near Fort Wayne, and the Reinhards were very religious. The Mennonites are literalists about the Holy Scriptures, and the Scriptures are the final authority on their way of life.

Keith was four years old and his brother was two when their father, an upholsterer, died at home from complications of influenza. He had only $1,000 in life insurance, and Agnes Reinhard received $92 a month from the government. The young mother went to work as a clerk in the local grocery store and took in boarders for the top floor of their plain white frame house on the edge of town. Keith's grandparents came back from Fort Wayne to live in Berne when Keith started school, and his grandfather was a very important influence in his life. He also helped out the family financially.

"I was sure that what happened was in the plan of our lives," Agnes Reinhard says. "The boys never suffered. They always had all they needed."

The Reinhard boys were brought up in the Mennonite church a few blocks away from the house, attending Sunday school regularly and singing in the chorus.

The church was "quite strict in those days," Mrs. Reinhard explains. "There were rules about who people married and rules against dancing." Drinking and smoking certainly were out of the question.

The boys had all kinds of odd jobs, starting early by pulling weeds on a truck farm. In high school Keith took a job assisting a photographer in town and built a darkroom in the basement at home. He drew well and wanted to buy art supplies, but there was nowhere in Berne to find them.

As high school came to an end, Reinhard won a Rotary International scholarship to a design school in Indianapolis, but it was closed down during the McCarthy era, Reinhard says, and Rotary withdrew its scholarship offer. Keith's aunt offered him money to go to either Bob Jones University or Wheaton College, both of which were religious schools. Reinhard says he couldn't accept the offer on those terms.

Not having gone to college still haunts Reinhard today. His friends say he feels inadequate because of his lack of a formal education. He relentlessly tries to accumulate information about art and music and cultural history.

Breaking away from the restraints of Berne meant going to Fort Wayne and taking a job in a commercial art studio. "I didn't have a career path," Reinhard says, "I was just happy to have a job." He married in his early twenties, and Jackie and Keith Reinhard soon had their first child. At the time Keith was working at the Magnavox Co., where he had a low-profile job in the advertising and communications department.

The growing Reinhard family then moved to Bloomington, Illinois, where 29-year-old Keith was employed by an ad agency called the Biddle Co. There he worked on State Farm Insurance, which was to become another of his trademark accounts.

The same week in November 1963 that John F. Kennedy was shot, Reinhard's grandfather died. The impact on Reinhard was such that he found himself in the hospital suffering a nervous breakdown.

The counseling he received during his two-month hospital stay also revealed to Reinhard a deep-seated lack of self-confidence.

"I told the psychiatrist I didn't feel I was any good at advertising," he says. "He asked me how long I had been doing work associated with advertising, and I said, 'Ever since high school.'

" 'Well, you're a better judge than I am,' " the psychiatrist replied, according to Reinhard.

Prior to his hospitalization, Reinhard had been interviewed for a job at Needham Harper and Steers. Says Reinhard, "When I was in the hospital, I wrote to the person who had interviewed me, saying I was sure that he didn't want me to work for him now." But he also mentioned the date in January that the doctor said he would be ready to return to work. On that day, he got a call from Needham, and the representative from his prospective employer asked, "How do you feel?"

It was the vote of confidence Reinhard needed to get back on his feet, and shortly thereafter the young adman moved his family to Chicago.

Although Reinhard had been an art director in his previous jobs, Needham wasn't interested in his talents in that area. He became the oldest junior copywriter on beginner's row. "I sat next to the pop machine and made change all day and wrote at night," he says.

Needham had the account for State Farm's national advertising, the same company Biddle handled for the smaller regional business.

"I thought I could fake it by writing little ads," Reinhard says. "I knew about ten words about insurance.

"My first assignment was to write twenty-six humorous radio commercials, and I had no idea what to do. So I took out all kinds of comedy records from the library. And I would write all night. When I was sure the commercials were funny, I'd walk down the hall to the creative director's office, and then without going in, turn around and go rewrite them."

"He's a combination of idealist and perfectionist, which is a problem at times," says his colleague Joel Hochberg. "When you have both, you're never satisfied. It could always be better. It's never perfect, but he feels it should be perfect. He never can achieve the ideal."

The McDonald's account was like a monster that devoured advertising, and it provided Reinhard with the opportunity to display his talents, especially for music.

"You deserve a break today" was the theme, with song and dance sequences like Hollywood production numbers. Side by side with associate creative director Dan Nichols, Reinhard wrote and produced McDonald's commercials by the score. Friends in the creative department would often come into the office early in the morning and find Reinhard at his desk typing. He had been there all night.

"I picked him up from the carpet once just after he'd turned down some of my ideas," Nichols said. "He wasn't eating right, wasn't going to lunch. He went to the hospital for tests and was back in the office the next day."

But by 1975 the McDonald's system was tiring of giving Americans a break, and Fred Turner and the top marketing brass were ready for some new advertising from Needham. It became a question of "deliver now, or we're moving the account."

Blair Vedder, Needham's top man, wanted to have a "gang-bang," throw the project open to everyone in the agency. But Reinhard persuaded Vedder to allow him and Dan Nichols to hole up for a week in the Drake Hotel in New York to come up with the answer.

The duo went in with twelve different strategies from which sprang twelve different ad campaigns. Surrounded by half-eaten hamburgers and empty Heineken bottles, they wrote script after script. They assigned musical projects to the top jingle writers in Manhattan, including the prominent Sid Woloshin.

Woloshin's assignment was a love song. The fast-food experience had become too impersonal, the strategists decided, so Reinhard wanted to focus on the individual. "You're the one . . . you're the only reason," he had written.

Once in the studio, they recorded many versions of the love song to the McDonald's customer. But singer Ginny Reddington contributed the touch that made it a winner. When she sang the lyrics, she added the extra "you."

"You, you're the one," emerged the favorite of that frenetic week, and McDonald's executives approved production of the campaign.

Months of shooting and recording preceded the crucial meeting at the Civic Opera House in Chicago where the all-important McDonald's owner-operators would be brought together to respond to the new campaign. Reinhard and Nichols were in the editing suite until two in the morning that day, with McDonald's top marketing man Paul Schrage hanging over their shoulders. They knew that either the operators would love the campaign and Needham would keep the business or it could mean major trouble for the agency.

"You, you're the one" was a smash, and on the strength of this victory, in April 1975, Vedder asked the 40-year-old Reinhard to become the agency's director of creative services.

Reinhard told his boss he first wanted to discuss it with his wife. The couple then had five children, and the new job would mean a more extreme time commitment. Jackie gave her okay.

Now Reinhard had the chance to build the creative department of Needham, Harper and Steers into his own personal vision. Like the great creative men before him who built their own agencies, Leo Burnett and Bill Bernbach, Reinhard wanted Needham to be an oasis of creativity. He tried to foster an environment where the contributors had fun, made money, and took enormous pride in their work.

Because he had the clear backing of agency chairman Paul Harper, Reinhard's influence was greater than that of the businessmen who ran the account-service side of the agency. The extremely close ties between him and McDonald's gave him even more power.

Reinhard was trying to build Needham into a kind of Camelot, of which he would be the beneficent king. He also wanted the agency to be like a family, and he was the father to whom everyone came for inspiration and guidance.

In September, on Keith and Jackie's fifteenth wedding anniversary, as they were driving home to Evanston on Chicago's North Shore, Jackie told Keith their marriage was over.

"You'll have to see the children every weekend," she said to him, believing he would resist. Reinhard was taken totally by surprise. But his friends knew that Needham was the mistress who had stolen Reinhard from his wife. He had sacrificed his marriage to his company without realizing that by leaving town so often and spending so many late nights at the office, he was totally losing touch with his wife.

To his Mennonite mother in Berne, divorce was a disgrace. Agnes Reinhard, keeping the shame to herself, deteriorated physically because she couldn't eat or sleep.

A bright young account-service executive at Needham brought Reinhard back from the devastation he felt as a result of his divorce.

Rose-Lee Simons, in her early thirties, was the management supervisor on the McDonald's account, a powerful position in the company. A brilliant advertising strategist, Simons lacked confidence in her ability as a speaker.

As intense and snappish as Reinhard was slow-talking and deliberate, Simons, too, was dedicated to the agency and was an important part of the Needham family.

The night before an important presentation at McDonald's Oak Brook headquarters, she had a bad case of the jitters. As the top account person, it was up to her to kick off the show and set the stage for the main attraction, the commercials being shown for the client's approval.

"Why don't we do it as a team?" Reinhard suggested. They rehearsed late into the evening and then drove north from the city to a suburban restaurant for hamburgers. Just a few months later, Simons and Reinhard were married, and their powerful partnership strengthened Reinhard's belief in Needham as a creative family. The team remained intact, both in the office and in marriage, until Reinhard was named president of the advertising agency.

CHAPTER 8

Almost everyone who was a star at Doyle Dane Bernbach when it was the greatest advertising agency in New York says its death began when the company went public in 1964.

Through the 1950s and early 1960s, the best copywriters and art directors in New York were eager to take pay cuts from their jobs at other ad agencies to toil until four in the morning under the tutelage of William Bernbach.

"Doyle Dane Bernbach was a great place to work if your parents could afford to send you there," they joked. Doyle Dane Bernbach made its reputation with witty, appealing, and totally original advertising that persuaded and made the sale through its ability to charm the prospect.

Bill Bernbach, a native New Yorker who got his real start at Grey Advertising and quickly was promoted from copywriter to copy chief to creative director, feared the loss of the artistic touch in the work emanating from Grey as it grew to become a major agency.

He voiced this concern to Grey management in a letter in 1947. "If we are to advance," Bernbach wrote, "we must emerge as a distinctive personality. We must develop our own philosophy and not have the advertising philosophy of others imposed on us.

"Let us blaze new trails. Let us prove to the world that good taste, good art, good writing can be good selling."

Just two years later, Bernbach, along with Ned Doyle, a vice-president and account executive at Grey, and Maxwell Dane, who was running his own small agency in Manhattan, broke away to form Doyle Dane Bernbach.

The agency made advertising history with its first client, Orbach's department store. Orbach's had been a client of Grey's, but it was not prospering. It needed an image revamp, and its owner turned to Bernbach.

"Liberal Trade-In. Bring in your wife and just a few dollars . . . we will give you a new woman," read the headline on one of the early ads. Bernbach repositioned Orbach's to a chic place for bargains and turned the company's business around. In the process, the agency created ads that have become classics. The annals of retail advertising are not complete without mention of the one ad that was most identified with Orbach's: A very female feline, wearing a chapeau and smoking a cigarette in a dainty long holder, tells the world how "I found out about Joan." Although poor Joan's husband was not the business success he appeared to be, she was able to be kept in "a mink stole and Paris suits" by shopping at Orbach's.

This fashion consciousness did not come naturally to Bill Bernbach. The man who worked more closely with him than anyone else, copywriter and creative director Bob Levenson, wrote that Bernbach was "slight, pale, unathletic and physically altogether unprepossessing." He was a "frail, five-foot-seven-inch, blond, blue-eyed, quick-witted package of ego, ambition, confidence, determination and energy," Levenson wrote in a book that was his tribute to his boss.

Bernbach's vision enabled him to attract some of the most talented people in the business to help him realize his dream.

Famous copywriters and art directors, such as Levenson, Bob Gage, Phyllis Robinson, and Helmut Krone, joined him and stayed on loyally. Others, such as George Lois and Mary Wells, found Doyle Dane Bernbach to be their training ground and eventually went off to launch famous ad agencies of their own.

The people who joined Bernbach at the beginning were in love with advertising. They didn't like the political machinations of bigger shops and wouldn't tolerate the trickery or compromises that were often standard at other agencies.

Instead they liked to think of Doyle Dane Bernbach as a flourishing shop of artists reminiscent of the Renaissance. Bernbach was like the patron who gave the artist the right and the resources to create. Rather than competing with each other, the writer-and-art-director teams would encourage each other, commenting on the work and spurring their colleagues to even greater achievements.

During the years of the late 1950s and early 1960s, these creative people brought to newspapers, magazines, radio, and television some of the most famous advertising in the American culture. They broke taboos, turned marketing disadvantages into strong selling points, and brought totally new products into the mainstream of American consumerism.

No one had introduced the question of ethnicity into a marketing strategy before Doyle Dane Bernbach told New York that "You don't have to be Jewish to love Levy's" Jewish rye bread.

When Americans were flocking to gas-guzzling Detroit-built automobiles to reflect their prosperity, Doyle Dane Bernbach had the audacity to suggest that consumers "Think small" and buy a Volkswagen. The innovative creators transformed the "bug's" size into a plethora of endearing qualities.

They tapped into the spirit of the '60s in an ad for the Volkswagen station wagon with an ad headlined "Do you have the right kind of wife for it?"

"Can your wife bake her own bread? . . . Will she say 'Yes'

to a camping trip after 50 straight weeks of cooking? Live another year without furniture and take a trip to Europe instead? . . . Let you give up your job with a smile? . . . And mean it? Congratulations," read the copy in one memorable ad for a shiny red and white minibus.

"Bernbach was the finest editor in the world," says Bert Steinhauser, a commercial director in New York who worked at Doyle Dane Bernbach for more than twenty years.

"It was like he had a divining rod. He would look at a campaign and say 'That is the one.' "

The revolutionary campaign for Avis car rentals, "We try harder," was the product of two DDB stars, Paula Green and Helmut Krone. The ads were strong and unusual-looking, with headlines such as "Avis can't afford dirty ashtrays" and the copy declaring that "When you're not the biggest in rent a cars, you have to try harder. We do. We're only No. 2."

"The account people hated the campaign," Green says. "They did research that showed that 50 percent of the people interviewed didn't like the campaign. We asked for Bill to come into the meeting. 'What about the other 50 percent? That's who we want to reach.' "

Passing by offices on the creative floor of the agency, Bernbach would respond to pieces of advertising the art directors and copywriters flashed at him. He could give the ad one look and comment on a word or a headline or a color that needed to be fixed. And weeks later, he'd remember the correction he suggested the next time he saw the ad, even if it was in a room full of work.

The creative reviews would take place in a conference room with a giant round table, because part of the Bernbach style was to generate the feeling of a democracy: There was to be no "head of the table." In the glory years of Doyle Dane Bernbach, it was the creative leader's decision that determined which ad campaign made the journey from the confines of the agency to the crucial meeting with the client.

Bernbach would choose the idea he thought was the best and "then he would touch it, make it his. It was part of his ego, so the work always became his," one of his early colleagues recounts.

And through this unique dedication to quality advertising came fame, not only for Bernbach but for his staff as well. The chief was elected to the Copywriters Hall of Fame, and so were his staffers Phyllis Robinson and Bob Levenson.

Choosing only one campaign and taking it to the advertiser with a strong recommendation was an aggressive way to run an advertising agency. And it brought about aggressive campaigns that endured for decades.

Polaroid invented the phenomenon of instant photography and went to Doyle Dane Bernbach, still in its formative stages, for advertising. Through the 1950s and into the 1960s, television's most popular personalities, from Garry Moore to Jack Paar to Johnny Carson, used the medium of live TV to demonstrate Polaroid pictures developing before your eyes.

Progressing from the simple demonstration method once the idea of the instant picture began to catch on, Doyle Dane Bernbach turned to consumers' emotions—the capturing of family love—to kindle the urge to buy an instant camera.

Always in step with the times and the mind of the consumer, Doyle Dane Bernbach also created the brilliant campaign featuring James Garner and Mariette Hartley, which appealed to the sharp, progressive young adult who was becoming the key target audience for consumer products in the late 1970s and early 1980s.

The pioneers at Doyle Dane Bernbach proved conclusively that dedication to superior advertising could bring success. From its birth in 1949, when the agency billed $775,000 and made $11,000 in profit, DDB continued to build its billings base, growing from $2.6 million in 1951 to $16.3 million in 1956 to $50 million in 1961. At the time management announced the company's intention to go public, it was having one of its hottest years, adding about ten new accounts and moving over the $100 million mark in billings.

DDB was the third New York agency to offer its shares to the public in the 1960s, following the lead of Papert, Koenig, Lois and Foote, Cone & Belding. At the time, Maxwell Dane told the advertising community that going public was a move to "establish a fair market value for the agency's stock and will also aid the agency in rewarding talent."

Clearly, however, it was a way for the people who started the companies to make major fortunes. Bernbach and his wife Evelyn, the Danes, and Ned Doyle owned the majority of the shares, and a small group of account service executives, copywriters, and art directors owned lesser amounts.

The first public shares were offered for about $25, and by the company's first annual meeting a year later, they had risen to more than $34, on increasing billings and revenues.

Bernbach set up what could have been an impediment to the agency's growth. Despite the fact that his partner Ned Doyle was a three-pack-a-day smoker, Bernbach decreed that in light of the Surgeon General's report on the harmful effects of cigarette smoking, his agency would never handle the advertising account of a tobacco company. Cigarette advertising was among the most profitable kind of account an agency could handle, but as long as Bernbach lived, his colleagues never challenged his stand.

Being the chief of a publicly held company gave Bernbach an even wider forum for his views, upon which he expounded at the company's first shareholders' meeting as well as at industry events around the country.

Among the ways an agency could grow, Bernbach told his company's shareholders in 1965, was through "social connections," "gobbling up things around you," as Interpublic had done, or "accounts brought in by a personality."

"We don't know anybody, so social connections don't help us," he said. "Merging is dangerous because we have a certain personality and merging might put a crack in that personality.

"If your ads are talked about, you will grow in the proper way. We're tricky that way. We increase sales for clients. If you make money for someone else, they forget all the firmness you exercise, all the toughness you've shown, and they remember that you made money for them."

International expansion became the next order of business for DDB, and by 1967 the agency had built up its offices in Dusseldorf, London, Mexico City, Montreal, and Toronto, increasing overseas billings by 80 percent.

But foreign ad agencies weren't the only places where DDB president Joseph R. Daly started putting the agency's money. Doyle Dane Bernbach was part of a group of investors that bought the Georg Jensen Inc. store in Manhattan. The relationship was public to the extent that the prestigious Jensen store, which sells silver jewelry and decorative objects, displayed a giant package of Alka-Seltzer during the Christmas selling season. Alka-Seltzer was one of DDB's new account wins in 1969.

The agency that had been dedicated to the creative product above all else, and yet was still tremendously successful, became as financially motivated as its counterparts on Madison Avenue, a factor that caused disillusionment among the most talented and committed of the creative staff. It was a maturation process that many of the Bernbach stars weren't eager to undergo. Bernbach had protected his agency flock as if he was the father and they were his children.

"We worked on ads from visceral feelings," says Bert Steinhauser, who became one of the top creative executives at DDB. "But the agency took an expansion route through supermarket products" and that resulted in the "invasion of the MBAs."

Another former DDB creative director traces the downfall of the agency to the acceptance of Procter & Gamble as a client. "They came to us for what we did," he says, "but instead of trying to be DDB doing P&G, we started to do things their way. It seemed a copout and was symbolic of the atrophy of principles. It truly was like a cancer beginning to grow."

"The most important thing used to be 'how good is the advertising?' " says Roy Grace, who was the top creative director at DDB for eight years. "Then it became 'we must not lose this business.' What was a place of great energy became an agency of second-guessing and worrying. Every quarter we had to have better numbers. It's like the Flying Wallendas—when you become too conscious of what you're doing, you're headed for a fall."

The numbers did keep getting better until 1972, when the agency lost about $30 million in billings. The next year brought the departures of H.J. Heinz and Polaroid's Cool-Ray business, as well as Uniroyal athletic products—followed by a knee-jerk reaction from management.

The agency tried to reposition itself as one that was as "disciplined" as it was creative by boosting executives from the account-management side to more powerful positions. This strategy resulted in a parade of five presidents in five years, several of them brought in from other companies, and all of them financially oriented rather than trained in the rarefied culture of Doyle Dane Bernbach's creative dedication.

The financial men, especially Neil Austrian who became DDB president in the late 1970s, began to look at agency acquisitions as the means to further growth and held talks with many shops, including Wyse Advertising and the hot Ally & Gargano agency. Neither of these deals ever came to fruition, but DDB did acquire smaller agencies, including regional firms such as the St. Louis agency Barickman Advertising.

Other acquisitions included Cargill Wilson & Acree in the

South, direct marketing agency Rapp & Collins, Milici/Valenti Advertising, and Briggs & Mitchell, all of them operated as separate profit centers.

International acquisitions also became a prime target, and by 1981, when DDB was billing close to $1 billion annually, management announced its intention to build a European network under the direction of the founder's son, John L. Bernbach.

Pan-European advertising was a trendy preoccupation in the early part of the eighties as multinational advertisers started planning for the day when satellite transmission of television signals would beam programming and advertising to sets across the continent. DDB wanted to join in the trend for clients such as Polaroid and Volkswagen, who were indicating their interest in an agency's overseas strength.

On the surface, the agency continued to post incremental growth, with billings increasing by as much as $100 million annually through new business and acquisition.

Bill Bernbach's identity, meanwhile, got lost in the executive shuffle.

"He'd be walking down the hall and pull out of his pocket a letter from some obscure person who had written to say how great the agency was," Steinhauser recalls. "He needed this for reinforcement. He'd show it to you and as he was walking away you'd be saying to yourself 'Poor baby.' "

The closely knit family at DDB in New York was pulled apart by management's new attitudes. "By 1980, I came to work each day in search of a business I used to work in," says one former creative director.

The great stars of the Doyle Dane Bernbach constellation, disillusioned with the environment, took off on their own. They became commercial directors, started their own small agencies, or took their credentials to competitive shops.

Clients apparently felt the same way. Though it is always difficult to pinpoint the exigencies of an advertiser that motivate its executives to move an account, the exodus from DDB in the early 1980s was dramatic. Some of the accounts on which DDB built its reputation began looking for the 1980s version of a "hot creative shop" to take its place. Levy's bread, one of the founding accounts, was acquired by another bakery, and the new owner moved the advertising business to its own agency, Isidore Lefkowitz Elgort.

A new executive lineup at Avis Rent A Car was romanced by BBDO International, and the entire $20 million Avis account was yanked from DDB.

American Airlines, which under DDB's creative leadership developed the well-known campaign "Doing what we do best," moved its headquarters to Dallas, making a working relationship with a New York agency logistically difficult. Bozell & Jacobs won the $45 million account, and DDB picked up Pan American World Airways instead. But that relationship lasted less than a year, and Pan Am switched to Wells, Rich, Greene.

Sadly, at the same time, Bill Bernbach began his quiet battle with leukemia that would take his life in 1982, when he was 71. In retrospect, many of the agency's former executives believed that not planning for a smooth succession was another key factor in the agency's demise. Of all the creative executives who served Bernbach during his glory years, neither Bob Levenson nor Marvin Honig nor Roy Grace nor any of the others who might have been successfully groomed to assume his mantle was given the proper authority or experience to succeed in the battle with the financial men in power.

Bernbach had the power and respect to make the account management team see the creative person's side of the story and to push through the unique advertising that had built the agency's reputation. As he withdrew from the daily operation of the agency, which had by this time grown to more than 2,800 employees around the world, the schism between the ego-driven creative powers and the account managers expanded until it was too wide to bridge.

Chairman Joseph R. Daly and president Neil Austrian saw the future of DDB as being part of a larger whole. "There's no question but that the largest agencies, as a group, are continuing to increase their market share at the expense of the medium-size agencies," Austrian said at the company's shareholders meeting in May 1982. "This is happening because most of the large budget increases are coming from multinational clients who are assigning their accounts, with increasing frequency, to the large multinational agencies."

Daly and Austrian wanted to be part of that trend and began holding merger discussions with representatives of several agencies. Many suitors, including Saatchi & Saatchi, were entertained, but the one deal that came within an inch of being signed was with Foote, Cone & Belding, the Chicago-headquartered publicly held shop.

FCB was an agency whose background and reputation could not have been more different from that of Doyle Dane Bernbach. While DDB got its start by welcoming spirited people who were Jewish and Italian, and educated or not, as long as they had talent, FCB was identified with a rather bland, white-bread professional style.

Under its longtime chairman Arthur Schultz, FCB was often described as an agency that just as easily could have been a bank. It was said to be incidental that the product the company was selling happened to be ads rather than financial instruments. Creative staffers were prohibited from decorating their office walls with the crazy posters and other wacky decorations that were commonplace and part of the environment at just about every other ad agency. Even drinking coffee at one's desk was prohibited.

Early in 1982, Norman W. Brown was installed as the new

chief executive officer. "We were an agency of the heartland," said the soft-spoken, undemonstrative agency chief. "One that was straight, unflamboyant and solid."

But Brown realized that the agency's ailing creative reputation could be perilous. In the first three months of his tenure, he said, "reestablishing creative excellence was a top priority. Doyle Dane Bernbach was one option of how to fulfill that."

Doyle Dane Bernbach, on the other hand, was in dire need of the management strength of the midwestern company. And together, they believed, the two agencies could build the international network that was becoming so important in the competitive marketplace.

But as disparate as the two companies' cultures were, nothing could have divided them more than the issue of cigarette advertising, which had always been an issue on which Bernbach would not compromise. One of Foote, Cone & Belding's biggest accounts in New York was Lorillard Inc.'s Kent cigarette brand.

Although there was heartfelt resistance from some members of the board, just months before Bill Bernbach's death his executive team, led by Neil Austrian and Roy Grace, swiftly decided to toss away his long-held policy in order to merge with the ill-matched FCB.

"We loved the look of it on paper," Norman Brown said. "Their strength, geographically and creatively, combined perfectly with our greater strength in marketing." DDB was growing quickly in Europe and had a strong presence in New York, while Chicago and West Coast operations were prospering. The managements of the two companies had explored merger possibilities four or five years earlier, but now the time seemed to be just right.

"It was right at a moment in history that we had identical revenues, billings size and market share," Brown said. "We were No. 9 and 10 in the rankings and together we would create the biggest agency in the U.S."

The FCB team, led by Brown, met in New York with Austrian and Grace to draw up the final merger papers. Many of the complicated issues in creating a merger of the two firms, which together would have billings in the $2 billion range, had been resolved. The two agencies would have been integrated into one, with Doyle Dane Bernbach remaining the dominant force in New York. The New York office of FCB, which was headed by John O'Toole, would have been folded into DDB. In the rest of the country, FCB would retain its operations, incorporating DDB offices on the West Coast. Market-by-market consolidations were planned in the rest of the world.

The meeting continued into the night, and the participants began to understand that no matter how good it looked on paper, the underlying question remained: Could these sharply different cultures be manageable under a single agency?

Brown and his team realized they would not be able to subjugate the ego-driven DDB execs into their management style. "We're pulling back," Brown told Austrian.

The issue that came to symbolize the difficulty was that after wrestling with an infinite number of permutations of Foote, Cone & Belding and Doyle Dane Bernbach, the negotiating teams could not agree on a name.

CHAPTER 9

The biggest financial scandal in the history of the advertising industry broke on a bone-chilling February afternoon in 1982 with a terse statement from Don Johnston, the chairman of publicly held JWT Group, the parent company of one of the country's oldest and most-respected ad agencies.

"In connection with our annual review of operations," Johnston said, "our accounting department determined that certain aspects of internal record keeping in our JWT syndication unit were handled improperly."

That announcement led to disclosures of computer manipulations, phony revenues, a restatement of four years' worth of earnings, and a $30 million write-off that first brought to the public eye the question of financial controls and executive responsibility at J. Walter Thompson Co.

In 1974, when Johnston was named chief executive officer of the 96-year-old Thompson company, it led the industry in worldwide billings and brought in revenues of close to $130 million. When the average American thought of an advertising agency, J. Walter Thompson was the one that came to mind. Thompson executives prided themselves on their sound relationships with clients that traced back to the beginning of the century.

The consumer-products giant Unilever had been with the New York office since 1902, and Kraft Inc. signed on with the Chicago office in 1922. For decades, holiday television specials, interrupted by Kraft commercials that would demonstrate myriad uses of Miracle Whip salad dressing, were produced by JWT.

Heartwarming commercials for Eastman Kodak and the qualities of its photographic products had been created by Thompson's New York office since 1930.

"I wish I were an Oscar Mayer weiner," the kind of advertising jingle that finds its way into the mind of every American consumer, came from the Chicago office of JWT, which first started working for Oscar Mayer & Co. in 1957.

At age 48, Johnston, physically unimposing but trim and athletically built, surprised the company by being appointed the successor to chairman Dan Seymour. Seymour was only the fourth chief executive officer in JWT history, and was the one who took the agency public in 1969, offering 790,000 shares of stock at $38 a share. The 1960s were boom times for Madison Avenue, and JWT was no exception as billings rose to $740 million by the end of the decade.

JWT developed a reputation for solid, conservative advertising and for keeping clients happy. The Thompson culture stressed client service of the old style. The management team liked to impress clients with the agency's resources, which ranged from a staff of social science professionals available for consultation to an authentic colonial dining room at the JWT headquarters in the Graybar Building.

As the first U.S. ad agency to open a foreign office—the move in 1890 to London—JWT in its glory days used the international circuit as a training ground for its up-and-coming executives.

A foray to London or Latin America was seen as part of the route to the top, and Don Johnston made the most of his foreign assignments. Following his graduation from Michigan State's school of journalism, he started his career as a trainee in JWT's Detroit office. Johnston received a company scholarship to Johns Hopkins and took a master's degree in international economics at the university's School of Advanced International Studies. He was assigned to JWT's New York office as an account executive but soon received his first foreign posting to Bogotá, Colombia. It was there he met his petite Latin American wife Sarita, known in the Johnstons' New Caanan, Connecticut, social milieu for her sharp financial mind and tough tennis game.

Johnston, a former marine who retains his erect posture and fastidious appearance from his military years, inherited a company that had just lived through a two-year period of account losses resulting in depressed earnings.

At the same time as he exerted profit pressure on his managers, Johnston changed the structure of the company from a giant ad agency to an even bigger holding company, of which he was the undisputed king. Backed with strong support from the JWT board, Johnston increased the company's holdings to include the world's biggest public relations firm, Hill & Knowlton, and one of New York's hot creative ad agencies, Lord Geller Federico Einstein. He created the holding company JWT Group to control all of the subsidiaries and took the title of chairman. The outside directors, including Gordon T. Wallis, the retired chairman of Irving Bank Corp., Walter D. Scott, former chairman of IDS/American Express Inc., and David L. Yunich, retired vice chairman of R. H. Macy & Co., were tremendously loyal to Johnston, who presented himself and his company as paragons of integrity and leadership in the advertising business.

But Johnston was out of touch with the times and with the realities inside his company. In the first six years of his reign, JWT lost its number-one ranking of U.S.-based agencies to privately held Young & Rubicam. Johnston's publicly stated priority was to make the JWT "brands"—the advertising agency, Hill & Knowlton, and the company's research subsidiary—the leaders in their fields. But other agency chief executives knew that marketers were putting more and more of their budgets into disciplines other than media advertising and public relations. Direct marketing, sales promotion, and specialized fields, such as health care marketing, were attracting the attention of Johnston's peers at other giant companies that were diversifying to add to their revenue base and profitability.

Johnston, instead, set often unrealistic profit targets for his managers, who were rewarded financially for the profitability of their individual units. The focus on profits diverted attention from what had always been the strong point of JWT: if the gentlemanly agency did not always deliver superior advertising, it could be counted on for making its clients feel they were getting superior service.

A symptom of this profit pressure came to light in 1978 when the venerable JWT was publicly embarrassed by the revelation that its biggest client, Ford Motor Co., was the victim of a double-billing scam of significant proportions. JWT shamefacedly had to repay Ford an undisclosed six-figure sum and apologize that its financial controls were not what they should be.

But this incident did not make Johnston pay closer attention to the operations of the J. Walter Thompson Co., of which he also was chairman and chief executive officer. Instead, with the establishment of the holding company structure in 1980, Johnston was pulled away from the advertising world and pushed to the financial community, where he was neither well-liked nor confident. Johnston took an almost adversarial position with securities analysts and the financial press, telling them what he thought they should hear and nothing more.

His relationship with the top management team was similar. When he did invite a colleague to lunch, it was usually a spartan affair at the Sky Club in the Pan Am Building. He developed a reputation as an instigator of the political maneuverings among his top managers, pitting one against the other as they jockeyed for key appointments. Starting a pattern that would soon emerge as the Johnston revolving door, one of the agency's most experienced executives, Wayne Fickinger, who had been president and chief operating officer of the worldwide agency J. Walter Thompson Co., left suddenly at the end of 1981, saying he was taking early retirement at age 55. Fickinger was known to have clashed openly with Johnston and, despite his management successes, could not see eye-to-eye with his boss. A few years later Fickinger reentered the agency business as one of the top executives of Bozell & Jacobs (now merged to become Bozell, Jacobs, Kenyon & Eckhardt), where he remains as vice chairman.

Johnston added to the top-heavy management framework by establishing JWT/U.S.A., a company that oversaw the strong offices of New York, Chicago, Detroit, D.C., San Francisco, and Los Angeles as well as smaller operations in Washington, Atlanta, and a string of field offices that worked on the giant Burger King account. A former creative director who had been in the New York office since 1972, Burton J. Manning, was named chairman of JWT/U.S.A., with the charge of improving the agency's reputation for prize-winning, attention-getting advertising.

The prestigious post was a long way from the poor Jewish neighborhood in Chicago where Manning grew up. The bearded, often rumpled writer did much to hide his origins for fear the truth would be a handicap to him in the conservative JWT culture. Manning never went to college. He wanted to be a writer, and spent his post-high-school years living in what he describes as a "garret" on the city's north side, experimenting with plays and prose. Manning earned the spending money he needed—and learned about salesmanship—hawking Encyclopedia Britannica door-to-door. His first job in advertising was as a copywriter at Leo Burnett Company, where he often stayed at his typewriter into the night, trying to outlast another young writer, Norman Muse, who would eventually become Burnett's chairman.

While at Burnett, Manning took credit for the famous campaign "When you're out of Schlitz, you're out of beer," which laid a foundation for his climb through the creative ranks. He moved down Michigan Avenue, Chicago's advertising boulevard, to JWT in 1967, and his ambition to climb to the top took root.

By the time Manning made it to the top of the U.S. company, still a bachelor in his late forties, he had built a reputation as an ambitious, work-obsessed creative man who had room for little else in his life.

Putting a creative director at the top of the company was a sound strategy on the part of Johnston, and it worked. The talented people who made the advertising had a rallying point, and JWT began to figure in the Clios, the New York Festivals, and other awards programs that hype the reputations of the Madison Avenue shops. With Manning at the helm, new business pitches had an effective editor and star who would jet to the city where the pitch was being held the evening before and jump into the frenzied activity. After the local team had worked for weeks on their presentation, Manning would review it and often make drastic changes, calling for all-nighters on the part of the staff to make it match his standards. The legend goes that Manning would then go off to bed, calling for a very early morning meeting before the pitch, which he would lead.

Although today Manning claims credit for the U.S. company's financial success in the years between 1982 and 1985, people who worked with him claim he had little interest in operational matters. As chairman, Manning tried to institute a compensation system under which managers would be rewarded according to the quality of their unit's creative work. The system never really went into operation, but it led to the establishment of a creative standards committee, which reviewed the entire body of the agency's work for the first time.

Manning's first chief operating officer, Greg Bathon, who was pulled in from the international account management circuit when the U.S. company was formed, soon revealed he was not up to the job. By the fall of 1981, Johnston realized his selection of Bathon was a poor one and started making plans to replace him.

The first explosion came in the initial week of February 1982, with Johnston's carefully worded announcement about "financial irregularities" and the suspension of Marie Luisi, who headed the agency's syndication unit.

When JWT's accounting firm Price Waterhouse refused to sign off on the company's 1981 results, newly installed chief financial officer Herbert Eames took a tough look at some of the company's operations and discovered a morass of fictitious ledger entries in the section of the media department operations headed by Luisi.

In her post as senior vice-president and head of spot media buying and syndication, Luisi, known as "the Godmother" by colleagues and underlings because of her skill and power, oversaw all the time buying on local television stations, about $250 million worth of billings a year through JWT. Additionally, her unit produced syndicated programming, which was sold to the same local stations from which JWT bought time. So sometimes, instead of selling programs for cash, JWT would take in return from the stations chunks of time, which were put into a "time bank" in the agency's computers. The bartered time would be sold later to clients for placement of local commercials. The practice was called "barter syndication" and it was practiced by several of the big agencies in New York.

Just as the initial revelation of "improprieties" was being made public, Bathon, to whom Luisi's unit was responsible, resigned, though insiders still claim his departure was not directly related to the unraveling scam. Johnston replaced him as president and chief operating officer of JWT/U.S.A. with one of his most loyal followers, Walter J. O'Brien, who as executive vice-president and general manager of the Chicago office had boosted that operation's billings to the number-one slot in the JWT world. O'Brien had worked in the agency's European offices, and his close relationship with the CEO dated to Johnston's days in the international network. To take the place of the energetic and intense O'Brien in Chicago, Johnston installed 38-year-old Joseph W. O'Donnell, a blond, handsome hotshot who had earned his stripes on the Ford account in the agency's Detroit office.

Putting into operation the full power of the public relations arm Hill & Knowlton, Johnston, O'Brien, Eames, and the "special situations" team at the PR shop worked around the clock to communicate to its clients, at the same time that the word was going out to the financial community and the press, what they had found in their investigation of the "irregularities."

Two weeks after Johnston's initial statement, they announced that $24.5 million in "fictitious sales" had been entered into the syndication unit's computer, falsely boosting the company's revenues. Everything having to do with J. Walter Thompson sank into the doldrums. JWT Group's stock, which had been trading at an already depressed $22 per share, sank to about $16, and then to $14 per share. Morale at the agency in New York, newly ensconced in plush offices at the Park Avenue Atrium building, hit bottom as a widespread investigation pulled in staffers and clients alike. Midlevel managers were in the awkward position of having to defend the agency against the only half-joking banter of their counterparts at the client organizations.

In its barrage of material to the press and to its clients, Thompson insisted at the outset that no clients had been improperly billed in the falsifying of the sale of time in the "bank," but that did not stop several clients from sending in their own auditors to find out for sure.

The first week of April, JWT was forced to change its story again, admitting that two clients had been affected in the financial manipulations and that they would be reimbursed for the overbilling.

Even worse, the agency admitted, its initial estimates had been incorrect. Rather than $24.5 million in false entries, the write-off would total $30 million, to cover manipulations that had been going on since 1978. Net income for all of the years since then had to be restated downward, and earnings for the fourth quarter of 1981 dropped more than 43 percent because of the adjustments.

Johnston, in his statements to the public, placed the blame squarely and definitively on Marie Luisi. "It was the conclusion of the special investigation," he said, "that Marie Luisi was responsible for the improper activities enumerated above, as well as other improprieties. . . . As long as business depends on human beings, we will all be vulnerable to human frailty. We're not the first ones to discover that—we won't be the last. In today's world you are more than ever dependent on the personal integrity of the people involved."

The financial shenanigans sparked investigations by both the Securities and Exchange Commission and the Justice Department, neither of which has reached a conclusion. But rather than being lambasted by his board of directors for lack of proper controls, or being fired by his clients for running an agency in which such a scam could take place, Johnston made himself the object of sympathy. The company had been taken advantage of, he contended, by Luisi, a member of the agency's inside circle of managers who had spent twenty-four years at JWT, beginning as a secretary. Never was it suggested, however, that Luisi personally benefited from the inflated figures in her unit, except perhaps in the year-end bonus based on a performance that turned out to have been done with mirrors. It was determined that the syndication-unit computer people figured out how much a client would have to pay for a particular spot in the time bank and rolled the estimates into the active accounts entry at the end of the month, even though the time had not actually been sold.

Ironically, part of Johnston's strategy in this period of crisis, developed by the Hill & Knowlton team, was to make himself available to counsel JWT clients on how they could prevent computer-generated crime from being perpetrated at their own companies. And to make Johnston's position in the advertising industry even more difficult, it was during this tumultuous year that he was installed as the elected chairman of the prestigious American Association of Advertising Agencies at the group's annual conclave at the Greenbrier resort.

Luisi, who kept silent after she was discharged from the agency, claimed through her attorney—criminal lawyer Ivan Fisher who had recently become notorious because of his defense of convicted killer Jack Henry Abbott—that she had repeatedly written memos to Manning warning him of the problems with time banking. Manning, she said, ignored her missives.

One year later, Luisi came forth with her side of the story at the same time she announced she was filing a $125 million lawsuit against JWT and five of its top executives, including Johnston. Luisi said her case would be based on the combination of pressure from management for "big projections" and "a total lack of financial controls" at the company that made management responsible for creating a "breeding ground" from which the barter syndication scandal arose.

Luisi's complaint named Johnston, Manning, and Eames as defendants, as well as J. Walter Thompson Co. senior vice-president and treasurer Victor Gutierrez and her direct boss, Robert "Buck" Buchanan, executive vice-president and director of U.S. media.

Luisi charged that the defendants allegedly defamed her reputation and character and intentionally inflicted emotional distress on her in their accusations of misdeeds and her subsequent discharge from the company. JWT tried to get the suit dismissed, calling the allegations "ludicrous."

The initial lawsuit was dismissed by a New York state supreme court judge, but he gave Luisi the right to reopen the suit, which she did in mid-1984. The court ruled that Luisi did have a cause for action on a libel charge against both JWT and its chairman Don Johnston based on statements made by Johnston in press releases that accompanied her dismissal. The judge dismissed the claims against the other executives. Luisi's team of lawyers had been hopeful that the case would come to trial in the summer of 1987. But the New York state supreme court declined to hear the case, a ruling that is now being appealed.

"The Godmother" wasn't the only executive who took legal action against JWT and Johnston following the revelation of phony revenues and earnings. A well-known public relations executive in Washington, D.C., Robert K. Gray, was the top man in Hill & Knowlton's office there and a vice chairman when the firm was acquired by JWT in 1980. The deal was valued at $28.5 million, of which $13.6 million was paid to the owners of Hill & Knowlton in cash. Shares of JWT common stock, representing another $14 million, were also distributed as part of the deal. Gray's complaint was based on the contention that the executives of JWT who bought Hill & Knowlton presented a false picture of the agency's finances because the deal was based on 1979 results, which were restated downward following the disclosure of the phony revenues.

Gray believed that the top executives knew then about the trouble in the syndication unit and proved it when they sold large blocks of their personal holdings close to the time of the Hill & Knowlton deal. Six executives, including Johnston, Bathon, and Allen Jones, who was then chief financial officer, sold stock with values ranging from under $100,000 to close to $350,000, allegedly because of insider information. Gray's complaint said that an internal report by JWT's general counsel indicated there were questions about the revenues in Luisi's unit.

Robert Gray left Hill & Knowlton several months after the acquisition and established his own firm in Washington. His influence as a lobbyist grew even stronger through his close affiliation with the Reagan administration, for which Gray handled the first presidential inauguration.

In June 1986, Hill & Knowlton bought Gray & Co. Public Communications International Inc. for $21 million in stock, and the Gray suit was dropped.

Miraculously, both JWT and Johnston survived this imbroglio and emerged unscathed, at least on the surface. One year later, the agency's stock price had climbed back up to $33 a share. Another write-off of $10.7 million was taken for the closing of the controversial syndication unit, which caused another drop in net income to a mere $257,000 for 1982.

But largely due to the combined efforts of Manning and O'Brien, the New York office, which was hardest hit by the implications of the scandal, recouped and charged ahead. No clients defected, although Lever Bros. gave JWT a slap on the hand by taking away media-buying responsibility. Several new accounts were added, including R. T. French Co. for which JWT would create commercials starring talking sandwiches who loved French's mustard. The spots would win awards around the world. Burger King launched the historic battle of the burgers against McDonald's and Wendy's, taking fast-food advertising from the image-oriented strategies, which had been traditional, to a hard-sell, competitive arena.

And Don Johnston, nearing the age of 60, which had been established as the customary retirement age for executives in the J. Walter Thompson Co., began to scrutinize his management team as he thought about a plan of succession.

CHAPTER 10

The idea for Omnicom Group, the first three-way merger in the ad business, germinated during a Caribbean cruise, far away from New York or from any of the world capitals of adland that it would come to encompass.

Willi Schalk, the jet-setting head of BBDO's international group and a partner in its Dusseldorf agency Team/BBDO, was a guest of German publisher Axel Springer on the April 1985 maiden voyage of the luxury yacht *Sea Goddess*. Also part of the group of Springer's business associates on board was Juergen Knauss, a creative executive and managing director of Heye, Needham & Partner, the Munich-based West German operation of the American ad agency Needham Harper Worldwide.

The hard-driving Schalk, who since 1979 had been aggressively trying to strengthen the international operations of BBDO, was starting to turn around BBDO's fortunes overseas.

The Needham agency, on the other hand, was wrestling with growth and image problems in its New York office, and had yet to effectively tackle the worldwide arena. In Europe by early 1985, advertising executives already were taking seriously the "Snatch-it and Snatch-it" strategy of the Saatchi brothers and realizing that if their own networks were not strong, they would be easy prey for the Saatchis or another hungry agency trying to buy international capabilities.

Schalk, whose large horn-rim glasses give him a schoolboy appearance that he counters by alternately puffing on cigars or a pipe, turned a sympathetic ear to his countryman. The tall, ruddy, and well-muscled Knauss voiced his worries about the future of the Needham system in this changing environment. "In your case I'd be really concerned," Schalk said.

The Needham executive suggested that Schalk, who crisscrossed the Atlantic to New York with great frequency, have a discussion with Keith Reinhard, who had succeeded Paul Harper the year before and been named chairman and chief executive officer of the agency he renamed Needham Harper Worldwide. Perhaps Reinhard would be interested in a marriage to shore up his company for the future.

That discussion was the catalyst for the "Big Bang," a bombshell that made its impact right on Madison Avenue on Sunday, April 27, 1986, as its creative engineers met the press from suite 4108 in the Helmsley Palace. Starting early in the morning with *New York Times* columnist Philip Dougherty, whose article was deemed important enough to run on the paper's front page, the chief executive officers of BBDO International, Doyle Dane Bernbach Group, and Needham Harper Worldwide—Allen Rosenshine, Barry Loughrane, and Reinhard, respectively—personally contacted reporters throughout the day with the amazing news that their three agencies were coming together to form a new public holding company.

The company, which would be named Omnicom, was to be the biggest advertising group in the world, with billings of $5 billion. BBDO would operate as one network, Doyle Dane Bernbach and Needham Harper Worldwide were to be combined to form a second network, and the smaller subsidiary and specialty agencies of each bigger group would be managed by a third company called Diversified Agency Services.

Not only that, but the new company was to have a positioning other than its enormous size to differentiate itself from the other giant groups such as Interpublic and Saatchi & Saatchi. "Barry, Keith and I," Rosenshine said in the announcement, "all came to the conclusion that this megamerger of highly creative, independently strong agencies would be a tremendously positive force in our business. We get the feeling that too many deals are being done just to build volume without enough attention to a real benefit or value-added strategy for clients. . . . We want to offer the greatest creative resource in the business. Creativity is our reason for being, our point of difference and our competitive edge. We want to be nothing less than advertising's global creative superpower."

The Omnicom architects managed to keep the negotiations, which had been going on in one form or another for eight months, almost a total secret. But when the Big Bang reverberated on Madison Avenue and Michigan Avenue on that summerlike Monday morning, it marked a turning point for the industry. As Kenneth Roman, president of the Ogilvy Group, said when he heard the news from Dougherty of the *Times*, "That takes the game to a new level."

BBDO International, a strong, well-respected, and creatively driven agency led by the brilliant Allen Rosenshine, had billings of $2.5 billion in 1985 and was number seven in the annual rankings by *Advertising Age*. Rosenshine, then 47, who had begun his career as a copywriter, set the standard for creative excellence in his agency through his challenging communications, both inside his agency and industrywide. A native New Yorker who was educated at Columbia, Rosenshine is known for his verbal virtuosity and strategic insight. As he moved from running the agency's creative department of the flagship New York agency Batten, Barton, Durstine & Osborn, to chief executive officer of the entire company, Rosenshine made sure that its creative reputation would be burnished by putting power in the hands of one of Madison Avenue's most dynamic stars, Phil Dusenberry.

The Pepsi-Cola Co. grew to challenge Coca-Cola through the appeal of Dusenberry's advertising, beginning with the musical and high-spirited "Pepsi Generation" campaign, which made viewers smile at the same time it brought sentimental tears to their eyes. Dusenberry also led the team that created the memorable "GE, we bring good things to life" commercials that in an ever-so-contemporary style related the General Electric tools of everyday existence to the families who use them.

Dusenberry is a small man, always perfectly dressed, who approaches each project with a soft-spoken style and total concentration. A bachelor at age 52, he devotes himself tirelessly to creating advertising for BBDO, yet somehow has time for other achievements. His love for baseball led him to turn Bernard Malamud's novel *The Natural* into a screenplay, which Robert Redford made into a popular movie. And Dusenberry also served on the Tuesday Team, an ad hoc group of advertising big shots who collaborated on the campaign to put Ronald Reagan in the White House for a second term. And for the presidential election of 1988, Dusenberry participated in the early advertising efforts of Republican candidates while still serving as the chairman and chief creative officer of BBDO.

The combined vision of Rosenshine and Dusenberry—leading BBDO to growth through creative excellence—was recognized internationally on the French Riviera in June 1985. Entered with thousands of other commercials from around the world was the Pepsi spot that depicted an archeology professor of the future guiding his students through the ruins of our present society. They examine mysterious relics, including a baseball and an electric guitar, and the professor is able to explain the quaint and amusing uses they served in the late twentieth century. One student picks up another object: a green glass bottle in the classic Coca-Cola shape. "What's this, Professor?" asks the bewildered student. "I have no idea," he replies. "Pepsi, the choice of a new generation," reads the message on the screen.

"Archeology," as the spot was called, won the Grand Prix at the Cannes International Advertising Film Festival, which gave it the distinction of being the best commercial in the world. It brought much recognition to BBDO and to the spot's American director-cameraman Joe Pytka, and the business fortunes of all the companies involved took off for even greater heights.

It was the combination of BBDO's business success and creative reputation that gave solidity to the three-way merger. In the five years preceding the deal, BBDO posted steadily increasing revenues, growing from $176.6 million in 1981 to $335.6 million in 1985. Net income grew steadily from 1981, when it was $13.8 million, to 1984's $22.6 million. The next year it showed a slight decline to $19.6 million. Because of the relative financial strength of BBDO, it was natural that Rosenshine become the president and chief executive officer of the holding company.

Doyle Dane Bernbach, since the dissolution of merger talks with Foote, Cone & Belding a few years earlier and the death of founder William Bernbach late in 1982, had undergone a difficult period. Alan J. Gottesman, a leading analyst of advertising and media company stocks with L. F. Rothschild, Unterberg Towbin Inc., described DDB as an agency "struggling for five years to resume its financial growth, getting weary, losing clients and staff and needed [sic] a shot of vitality." DDB's financial picture in 1981 was just about on a par with that of BBDO, posting revenues of $173.3 million and profits of $11.1 million. But as DDB's revenues continued to grow, albeit more slowly, to $216.6 million in 1985, net income plummeted to $5.1 million.

The continuing management shuffle at DDB had put Barry Loughrane at the top of the U.S. division following William Bernbach's death, and in 1984 he was named president and chief executive officer of the company. But Loughrane did not have the support of the few original DDB stars remaining at the company, and he had the reputation of being more interested in the business of the many restaurants he owned than in that of DDB.

John Bernbach, the son of the founder, who had spent most of his career in the agency's London operation, took over the top management role in the international division at the same time Loughrane was named CEO. The Bernbach family, led by another son Paul, saw the fortunes of DDB falling and was concerned about the value of its 20 percent stake. The family had sold its shares back to DDB, loading the agency with debt. Loughrane knew it was time to sell the company, and the predators, primarily Saatchi & Saatchi, were circling closely.

At Needham Harper Worldwide, meanwhile, Keith Reinhard, despite his talent and hard work, was having a difficult time. From the time he was named the Chicago agency's president in 1980, life began to change for Reinhard. He could no longer maintain the "family" feeling that had been so comforting and inspirational to the creative team in Chicago. Nothing demonstrated this better than the manner in which his second wife, Rose-Lee, who had been appointed one of the three top client service executives in the agency, was forced to give up her job.

The post of president, of course, called for all department heads to report to Reinhard, and that included Rose-Lee Reinhard. Jealousy, pettiness, and gossip began to grow at the Chicago office, giving rise to the allegations of "pillow talk" between Keith and Rose-Lee and damaging the careers of others. Complaints filtered up to Reinhard's boss, Blair Vedder, a close-to-retirement executive, who decided to take some action.

Reinhard says that at a board meeting, a new employee handbook that would make policy for the agency was to be voted on. The manual contained a new provision of which Reinhard says he was not aware. The rule stated that relatives, including married couples, could not be in a reporting position to one another at Needham Harper and Steers. Reinhard, like the others on the board, voted to pass the handbook, and the "Rose-Lee rule" went into effect. One of the Reinhards would have to leave the company. "I never had lost sleep over a business problem, but I stayed up many nights worrying about how we'd handle this situation. I was the single greatest obstacle to her career.

"Blair and Paul Harper did things in an old-fashioned way," Reinhard says. "They would shut their door and make a decision.

"I realized then that the Needham we built and loved, the one with a warm family feeling, didn't exist anymore. I'd have to build a new one."

The biggest impediment to Reinhard's plan was the sudden departure of the agency's biggest and most important account, the McDonald's Corp. With billings of $75 million, it made up one third of the billings of the Chicago office and was a work-intensive piece of business that occupied as many as one hundred people. Theories abound as to why McDonald's chairman, Fred Turner, despite his close friendship with Reinhard, decided to move the account down the street to the much bigger Leo Burnett Co.

Some people believe that Reinhard, who was so closely identified with the prize-winning campaigns, began to take too much credit for McDonald's success, prompting resentment from the management at the client organization. Others say that Reinhard's jump to president, and the time he had to devote to other clients' businesses as well as to operational problems, meant much less time for McDonald's, a fact that angered the executives who depended on him at the fast-food chain.

Still others believe that the simple truth was what Paul Schrage, executive vice-president and chief marketing officer, said at the time of the stunning announcement in October 1981. Schrage cited Burnett's "depth and track record to further strengthen our marketing and industry leadership." The extraordinary growth of McDonald's, which added close to 500 restaurants in 1981 to bring the total to 6,739, carried with it the need for a bigger agency with greater resources. Leo Burnett Co., the biggest agency in Chicago with 1,500 employees, was seen as being able to provide that depth and to accommodate the needs of the McDonald's organization, yet not be dominated by them. Burnett had worked for McDonald's in countries abroad, including Holland, Belgium, and France, and its management team had been persistently wooing the Chicago-based corporation's executives for years.

According to Reinhard, "It was the biggest failure of my business life.

"I was the only person who could have convinced them they would have been happier staying at Needham," Reinhard says. Knowing that trouble was brewing, he "tried to reach Fred Turner all that weekend, and he was not available. He was not available to me until that Monday, when it already was announced."

Reinhard, who had moved away from the Mennonite faith to become an Episcopalian, relates this experience to the story of Mary and Martha in the New Testament. As he explains it, Christ comes to visit a humble dwelling. While Mary sat at his feet and tended to him and listened to his stories, Martha puttered in the kitchen and didn't pay enough attention to him personally.

"While Needham was puttering in the kitchen making advertising, [Burnett chairman] Jack Kopp was tending to McDonald's."

After the loss of the McDonald's account, Reinhard liked to point out to those visiting his office overlooking Lake Michigan the toy cannon he kept pointed at Jack Kopp's office in the Prudential Building, just a block away.

Needham, a privately held ad agency, did not fire people after the loss of McDonald's, quite an unusual strategy for the ad business. Instead, Reinhard believed, he would keep the people on as long as he could and use their resources in an effort to win new business.

The first win came rather quickly with the addition of Sears, Roebuck & Co.'s apparel advertising, a $35 million account that also had a touch of show-business glamor. Top model Cheryl Tiegs was the first female star to pitch a Sears line of clothing.

Needham recovered from its loss and still showed steady revenue growth from $72.4 million in 1981 to $121.2 million in 1985, the year before the merger. The impact on earnings, however, was evident in 1982, when profits dropped from $3.2 million in 1981 to $1.9 million the next year. But by 1983, profits were back up to $4.2 million, and to $5.4 million in 1985.

During the difficult year of 1982, Reinhard was named chairman and chief executive officer of the agency's U.S. operations, which caused him to focus his attention on the troubled New York office. Reinhard realized that to have a strong U.S. company he had to build a presence in New York. But for the midwestern-based Needham executive, New York was an enigma. Reinhard and his wife and baby daughter retained their million-dollar apartment in Chicago's new elegant high rise, One Magnificent Mile, but the agency chief was spending most of his time in New York.

On his arrival that summer, Reinhard threw a "Great Gatsby" party at the Water Club on the East River for the entire office. As the host, he was attired in a white suit, and during dinner he surprised his guests by taking the microphone from the band leader and belting out a rendition of "New York, New York."

But midwestern-style boosterism didn't fly in Manhattan, either with the staff or the clients. People at the agency snickered over Reinhard's weekly "Any Wednesday" memos, which offered homely words of wisdom or creative inspiration. And, with the exception of Al Wolfe, the executive Reinhard recruited to run the Chicago operation, the Needham chief had trouble finding strong managers who were willing to be subjugated to his own style.

Winning new business for the New York office became the top priority for Reinhard, who brought in one of his creative stars from the Chicago office, Tony Vanderwarker, to help with his expensive and time-devouring project.

The biggest account of the New York office was Xerox Corp., which Needham had made famous for their charming and tongue-in-check commercials starring the humble monk Brother Dominic, whose arduous assignments from his superiors were made possible by the help of Xerox office machines.

The aggressive new business effort, especially the futile pitch against BBDO for the prestigious Polaroid account (which after firing Doyle Dane Bernbach spent an unhappy year with Ally & Gargano), alienated the clients that remained. In almost as dramatic a loss as McDonald's was to the Chicago office, Xerox pulled its $40 million account—one fourth of the New York office's billings—from Needham early in 1986, signaling the need for Reinhard to make a dramatic move.

Photo by C. Zumwalt.

Following months of planning, the architects of the Omnicom three-way merger meet at their lawyers' offices to sign the final documents. Seated, *left to right*: John Golden, Goldman-Sachs; Norm Campbell, BBDO; Willi Schalk, BBDO; Allen Rosenshine, BBDO; and Keith Reinhard, Needham Harper Worldwide.

Below, *left to right*, the top officers of the merged companies: Barry Loughrane, Doyle Dane Bernbach; Allen Rosenshine and Keith Reinhard.

Photo by Joel Markman, BBDO.

Photo by Arnold Adler, Crain Communications Inc.

Don Johnston inherited the biggest U.S.-based ad agency, J. Walter Thompson Co., when he took over as chairman in 1974. By 1986, the company had sunk in the rankings and was beset by financial problems and management turmoil. Despite Johnston's initial tough fight, JWT was acquired by the British company WPP Group in 1987, and Johnston was forced out.

Martin Sorrell, who as financial director of Saatchi & Saatchi Co. helped the brothers plan their acquisition strategy, started his own firm in 1986. The next year, as chairman of WPP Group, he launched the first hostile takeover in the advertising industry and succeeded in acquiring JWT Group, the holding company of J. Walter Thompson Co. and Hill & Knowlton.

Maurice and Charles Saatchi founded their advertising agency in London in 1970. This photograph from the mid-1980s is one of the few the Saatchis permit to be reproduced. Today, their advertising and consulting companies form the largest marketing communications conglomerate in the world.

Photo by Joyce Ravid.

Carl Spielvogel and William Backer founded Backer & Spielvogel in 1979, bringing with them years of experience in the Interpublic Group of Companies agencies and the Miller Brewer Co. account. They sold their agency to Saatchi & Saatchi Co. in 1986, and now head the company formed by the merger of their shop with Ted Bates—Backer Spielvogel Bates.

Burton J. Manning lost the management struggle to become chairman of J. Walter Thompson Co. after heading its U.S. subsidiary, and left the company for a partnership role in a small agency. Less than a year later, when JWT was sold to WPP Group, owner Martin Sorrell brought Manning back as chairman and chief executive officer.

Joseph W. O'Donnell was chief executive officer of J. Walter Thompson Co. for less than one year. In an attempt to push his boss Don Johnston from day-to-day control of the agency's holding company, O'Donnell was fired and publicly vilified by his former mentor. A few months later he was hired by the Saatchis to head their troubled William Esty Co. subsidiary as chairman and chief executive officer.

Robert Jacoby, shown here just after the sale of his agency, Ted Bates Worldwide, believes he is the richest adman in America. The sale of the company he controlled to Saatchi & Saatchi Co. brought him proceeds of $112 million. He was fired shortly after the deal, but in the arbitration of his employment contract with the Saatchis, he won a settlement of another $4.7 million. Jacoby says 1988 will bring him back to the business world.

CHAPTER 11

"**P**roject Stanhope," one of the negotiations' secret code names, began in September 1985 with a series of breakfast meetings between the rapid-fire New Yorker, Allen Rosenshine, and the slow-talking midwesterner, Keith Reinhard, at the Stanhope Hotel on Fifth Avenue across the street from the Metropolitan Museum of Art. Despite their activities in industry associations, the two did not know each other, and the meetings were designed to help them build a relationship and formulate the possibilities of combining the two agencies.

At the same time, and unbeknownst to each other, both Reinhard and BBDO's Willi Schalk were romancing the top officers of Doyle Dane Bernbach. Reinhard and his right-hand man John Bradstock, an Australian and president of Needham's international operations, had been meeting off and on with Barry Loughrane during the past few years as Needham's Reinhard sought ways to boost his New York presence.

Schalk, a high school dropout who puts business before everything else in his life, used the occasion of the fall 1985 London convention of the European Association of Advertising Agencies to launch discussions with John Bernbach, who was then ending his term as the association's president. "I stayed for two hours instead of two days," Schalk says, "just to get to Bernbach and say 'Maybe we should meet.' "

Through the winter of early 1986, BBDO's Rosenshine and Schalk were having parallel, secret, and frequent meetings with both Needham's Reinhard and Bradstock, as well as with Doyle Dane Bernbach's Loughrane and Bernbach.

A plan was developed between BBDO and Needham calling for the agencies to unite to form two separate networks in the U.S., but to blend together in markets abroad depending on each agency's strength in each market.

"Meanwhile," Schalk says, "I had learned that Needham and DDB had had their own meetings six months before. . . . It was quite clear we had reached a point where we had to say: 'Let's do it.' "

When early evening fell in Germany on Saturday, March 1, 1986, Schalk telephoned Rosenshine at his country house in Great Barrington, Massachusetts, where the BBDO chief executive was spending the weekend with his youthful wife Missy and their two young daughters. Both understood it was time to make a decision to bring these discussions to some sort of resolution. Simultaneously, Rosenshine and Schalk arrived at the same idea: "What if we bring all three of us together? If they're both interested in doing something with us, why not with each other?"

Schalk returned quickly to New York and arranged a luncheon with Reinhard and a dinner with his Doyle Dane Bernbach friends for the same day. Rosenshine and Schalk tested the idea of a three-way union with Reinhard and got an immediately enthusiastic response. They then informed John Bernbach and Barry Loughrane that a few more people would be joining them for dinner and then brought along Reinhard and Bradstock to open the three-way negotiations.

Booking rooms under assumed names at the Helmsley Palace, just up Madison Avenue from the BBDO offices, became a specialty of Willi Schalk, a ploy that made it possible for the executives to leave the meetings through different exits to avoid gossip about their having been seen together. Suite 4108 became the negotiating headquarters, but the six agency honchos also jetted to wherever it was most convenient for them all to meet, including Reinhard's Chicago apartment, the scene of a key session on Palm Sunday.

All through March, only two men from each agency had any idea of the plan to create the world's largest advertising company. And the problems they anticipated focused primarily on two issues: How many clients would they lose as a result of conflicting accounts, and how could they manage the financial execution of the deal?

As the giant advertisers themselves—Philip Morris and General Foods, RJ Reynolds and Nabisco Brands, Procter & Gamble and Richardson-Vicks—put into operation mergers that dwarfed those of their ad agencies, the problems of conflicts within agencies became more and more complex.

The negotiating team led by Rosenshine, Reinhard, and Loughrane plotted and diagrammed what they believed to be every possible scenario of how they could keep competing companies within their networks. Doyle Dane Bernbach worked for Nabisco Brands, one of Needham's biggest clients in Chicago was General Mills, and BBDO had millions of dollars worth of Quaker Oats Co. business serving as one of the foundations of its Chicago office.

The lucrative automotive business was even more of a troublesome area for the merger planners, because each agency in the triad had its own car account. BBDO valued its relationship with Chrysler Corp.'s Dodge car and truck division, Volkswagen/Audi was a worldwide account for Doyle Dane Bernbach dating back to the agency's early days, and the Los Angeles office of Needham Harper Worldwide created the very successful and well-liked "Honda. We make it simple." ads for American Honda.

The fortunes of Needham's Chicago office had been boosted considerably through its success with the country's number-one brewer, Anheuser-Busch, which had started there with one small brand, Busch beer, and increasingly entrusted the agency with more business. The success of Bud Light—from its dramatic introductory campaign of "Bring out your best" to the popular "Give me a light"—spoofs made Needham a candidate for future growth. During the time the merger was being planned, Needham was in contention for the Michelob account, which was in trouble at the Ted Bates agency. So clearly the existence of the $15 million Old Milwaukee account from Stroh Brewery Co. at BBDO's New York office was a conflict the executives would have to eliminate.

The goal, of course, was to make the deal with minimal account fallout. But the admen were in a tough position. Because of Securities and Exchange Commission regulations, the two publicly held agencies could not inform their clients of their plans without releasing news of the negotiations. And no one wanted to let the news hit the street in the current climate of merger fever.

Just two months before, in a brass and crystal ballroom of the Plaza Hotel, an internationally known business professor, Jagdish N. Sheth, addressed the American Association of Advertising Agencies' seminar on global communications. Sheth, from the graduate school of business at the University of Southern California, told an audience of hundreds of top agency executives that consolidation in the advertising business would quickly lead to three giant agencies controlling the dominant share of worldwide advertising business. By March 1985, the top eight advertising agencies had seen their share of the world advertising spending rise from 14 percent in 1979 to 20 percent. Because the ad business is "client driven," Sheth said, it will follow the globalization trend of the companies it serves. He pointed to the consolidation of the automobile, tire, and airline industries as examples of the giant companies remaining strong while the smaller ones are forced into specialization to survive.

Global clients would expect their agencies to provide "one-stop shopping"—the ability to offer marketing services of all types and of consistent quality around the world, the professor explained.

Furthermore, Sheth predicted that within five years only one of the top three worldwide ad agencies would be American owned.

The Saatchis, who had put one of the leading proponents of global advertising, Harvard professor Theodore Levitt, on their board of directors, were already moving in the direction of becoming a one-stop communications supermarket. Their acquisitions of public relations firms, research companies, and consulting business gained momentum late in 1984. Saatchi holdings had grown to include the Rowland PR firm and the well-respected New York market research group Yankelovich Skelly & White. Its biggest acquisition outside of the advertising world had been the $100 million deal for the Hay Group, a Philadelphia-based management consulting firm.

Based on a stunning financial performance in 1985—with pretax profits rising 121 percent to $50.2 million—Saatchi & Saatchi, in April 1986, raised $600 million in a rights issue.

The Saatchis first dipped into their "war chest" to buy Backer & Spielvogel, which had been thriving as an independent agency despite the recent loss of one of its founding accounts, the ailing Miller High Life beer brand, to J. Walter Thompson Co.

While on a London trip in connection with client business in January, Spielvogel, chairman of the business committee of the Metropolitan Museum, arranged a meeting with Charles Saatchi, one of the world's most prominent collectors of modern art. So vast is the Saatchi collection that Charles opened a private gallery on Boundary Road in a North London neighborhood, not far from his home in St. John's Wood. The collection was started in 1970, as Charles and his American wife Doris began acquiring works by Minimalist artists. The gallery, a renovated paint warehouse with 27,000 square feet of exhibition space, has rotating shows that display only a small part of the collection, concentrating on just a few artists. Works from the Saatchi collection are also on display in museums around the world. Spielvogel sought Charles's participation as an international member of his museum committee. As Spielvogel tells it, Maurice entered Charles's office at the end of their discussion and brought up the subject of a merger deal.

Despite frequent avowals that he and his partners were not for sale, the Backer & Spielvogel management, which controlled billings of $385 million, were persuaded by the Saatchi's $50 million cash offer and the promise of as much as another $54 million due in future years based on performance.

Spielvogel said at the time that he was afraid his agency's lack of international resources would lead to the loss of major accounts. He explained that when his client Philip Morris Co. took over General Foods, people at his agency were "rubbing their hands with glee" at the "long-term opportunity to go to work for General Foods." But, he said, his competitors, the "900-lb. gorillas"—giant agencies such as Young & Rubicam and Ogilvy & Mather—probably had the advantage and could leverage their positions as General Foods agencies to pilfer the Philip Morris business from Backer & Speilvogel.

Saatchi & Saatchi also put together New York agency Dancer Fitzgerald Sample, known for its offbeat "Where's the Beef?" campaigns for Wendy's hamburgers, with its British Dorland's subsidiary to form a second network under the Saatchi banner. The hungry Saatchis saw the DFS deal as a way to increase their already considerable billings with the important multinational marketer Procter & Gamble, already strongly tied in to the Saatchi & Saatchi Compton network.

Also in pursuit of this goal, Maurice Saatchi was extending dinner invitations to a slim and stunning Chicago woman in her late forties, Charlotte Beers. As one of the rare female chief executive officers in the U.S. advertising world, Beers, along with her partner, second in command, and constant companion William Younglaus, headed Tatham-Laird & Kudner, a $235 million agency.

Headquartered in the same prestigious marble tower where both Beers and her industry colleague Reinhard kept apartments, TLK worked for several blue-chip clients, including Procter & Gamble. Beers, who keeps a trace of a Texas drawl despite having spent most of her career at the Chicago office of J. Walter Thompson (where people say creative director Burt Manning proposed marriage and was rejected), was eager to parley leadership of the medium-size agency into a bigger role. By selling to the Saatchis, Beers believed, she would be in a position for a top U.S. or even international job in the Saatchi organization. The high price tag TLK's partnership established for the agency's shares was one hitch in the negotiations.

But the biggest problem the Saatchis were encountering were the objections from its all-important client Procter & Gamble, whose advertising chief Robert Goldstein made clear his distaste for the idea of P&G billings at one of his chosen agencies being snatched to be controlled by the Saatchi brothers.

Doyle Dane Bernbach became the next target of Saatchi & Saatchi, and the hit men sent from London headquarters secretly stalked the vulnerable agency with the prestigious name. With the exception of Backer & Spielvogel, Saatchi & Saatchi's U.S. acquisitions did little to embellish the agency's creative reputation and were not in the same league creatively with the flagship agency in London.

Earlier advances by the Saatchis—whose acquisition team then was led by Martin Sorrell—were rebuffed by chairman Neil Austrian and his chief financial officer Robert Pfundstein. The independent, New York–centered DDB board didn't feel comfortable with the aggressive Saatchi style, nor did they believe Sorrell's promises of autonomy. John Bernbach, from his post in London, however, had a high opinion of the Saatchi & Saatchi agency there and was in favor of the merger deal. He assembled an influential group at the agency that included Bob Levenson, DDB's vice chairman and chief creative officer, to dine in New York with Martin Sorrell in an attempt to turn around the negative impression that the Saatchi financial men had created with his company's management. Maurice and Charles Saatchi remained aloof from these negotiations and refrained from even putting in a telephone call to founder Bill Bernbach, who then was still active in the company, to try to get his support. This small gesture could have swung the deal in the Saatchis' favor.

But by 1986, with accumulating account losses and major staff cuts outwardly reflecting the agency's weakening position, DDB's survival depended on a merger, and the board of directors knew it. The Saatchis, sensing vulnerability, called in a favor from a former key player in the DDB world who had since become one of their own. This time, the Saatchis and their American chief Anthony Simonds-Gooding enlisted the aid of Bob Levenson.

The continuing management turmoil at Doyle Dane Bernbach in the early 1980s had been too much even for Levenson, the copywriter and creative director who grew up at Bill Bernbach's right hand. His close relationship with his boss developed into his becoming practically part of the Bernbach family, a slightly older uncle to Paul and John Bernbach. But as others usurped his power after Bernbach's death, there was little left for Levenson at his old shop. In 1985 he was seduced by the promises of Maurice and Charles Saatchi, who said they were committed to improving the creative product of their New York flagship agency, Saatchi & Saatchi Compton.

Compton's work was an embarrassment to the brothers, whose promotional efforts in London continued to claim that Saatchi & Saatchi was a creative powerhouse. But in New York, lackluster testimonial commercials for products such as Johnson & Johnson's Tylenol looked as if they came from another decade. The dominance of the Procter & Gamble account—with hundreds of millions of dollars in billings based on Tide, Ivory Liquid, Crisco, Duncan Hines, and Folgers—brought in the dollars but also heckles when the ads were entered in international festivals. Levenson, buoyed by vows from top management in London that he would be free to invest in high-priced talent and to run the creative operation his way, signed on as vice chairman and chief creative officer.

As the Saatchis were putting together their deal for Doyle Dane Bernbach, Levenson, already disillusioned at his new job, was in the awkward position of aiding his new bosses in their takeover attempt. He was asked to draw up a list of key executives whom the Saatchis would sign to iron-clad contracts if the deal went through. The board, now led by Barry Loughrane, still included the influential Austrian and Pfundstein, who had not forgotten their unpleasant talks with the Saatchi team years earlier.

Just south on Madison Avenue, Rosenshine's team, too, was preparing to bring its plan to fruition.

For Rosenshine and Reinhard, who were determined to keep their intentions secret, one of the biggest challenges was to carry on agency business during regular working hours as if nothing was happening. The previous November, after the completion of consulting projects from Booz Allen & Hamilton and a team from the Harvard Business School, BBDO management had approved a new strategic direction for the company. It was promised then that the top management team would meet in Palm Springs in April to announce the new structure and the execution of that strategy.

The merger plans, of course, rendered the strategy moot, but Rosenshine and Schalk had to go through with the Palm Springs meeting as if they meant it. One element that might have raised suspicion, however, was that BBDO's top financial executives did not make it to Palm Springs.

In April, the chief financial officers of the three agencies— BBDO, Needham, and Doyle Dane Bernbach—were brought into the secret plan for the first time. "The assignment," they were told, "is not to argue. Now, please, get together immediately and work out a financial plan."

"A week later," Schalk says, "we came back from Palm Springs and they had worked out most of the details."

Reinhard, too, had to go against his straightforward style and finagle some fancy excuses for why his chief financial officer, Edward A. Haymes, didn't join the board members from around the world at the regular Needham Harper Worldwide spring directors' meeting on Saturday, April 19, in Los Angeles. Haymes had legal matters to handle, Reinhard said, to excuse the highly unusual absence. Although Reinhard, a very accomplished speaker and performer, did his best to conduct the meeting as if there were nothing exceptional taking place, his colleagues and friends could see he was preoccupied.

"One more thing," Reinhard said in closing. "We're having another board meeting Thursday in Chicago. Seven P.M. at the Ritz-Carlton."

Instead of lingering with his fellow officers, who had traveled from as far away as Australia and London for this meeting, Reinhard disappeared. So did Gerrold R. Rubin and Larry D. Postaer, the born-and-bred Chicagoans who headed Needham's Los Angeles office and ran the $58 million Honda account.

Honda, whose advertising had won honors in all of the major competitions, accounted for half the billings of the L.A. branch.

Reinhard led Postaer and Rubin to Rubin's spacious burgundy and beige office overlooking Wilshire Boulevard in Westwood and closed the door. The three settled into solid wing chairs in the corner to hear Reinhard's astounding news: The board would be asked on Thursday to approve the merger of Needham Harper Worldwide and Doyle Dane Bernbach Group to form one of the two agency networks under a new holding company that would also govern BBDO.

The low-key, down-to-earth West Coast duo was speechless as they quickly realized what this deal would mean to them. The architects of the merger had already decided that Rubin and Postaer's pride and joy, the Honda account, would have to be sacrificed to make the deal go through. Although Chrysler Corp. might be able to tolerate the presence of a competing car company as a client at a sister agency, there was no possibility of Honda and Volkswagen/Audi coexisting in what was to be called DDB Needham Worldwide. "Merger is not even a word in the Japanese language," Rubin said.

Reinhard presented Rubin, the account man, and Postaer, the creative director, with two alternatives. They could resign Honda, which would decimate the office and cause it to be merged with Tracy-Locke, a BBDO subsidiary with an office in L.A. Or they could split off on their own, and try to retain their clients in an independent agency.

"We had the potential of losing an awful lot," Rubin says. Neither Rubin, who was the first of the team to move to Los Angeles as head of the office, nor Postaer, who enjoyed his quietly successful life as a creative man with the additional perk of being able to play golf year-round in California, ever had designs on having their names on the door of an ad agency. They had, through a style that included solid work and little of the flamboyant showmanship of their boss Reinhard, built up the Los Angeles office client roster to include the California State Lottery, Home Federal Savings, and other well-known local advertisers.

They were comfortable, unpretentious, and scared.

After thoroughly discussing their situation with their startled wives over dinner on Saturday night, Rubin and Postaer had a Sunday breakfast with their accountant at the Westwood Marquis hotel, a popular rock-star and adland hangout near the U.C.L.A. campus. Their advisor essentially told them they'd be crazy not to take the chance. They were being offered a $100 million agency for $1.4 million, and they could use their stock in the holding company as collateral.

Rubin and Postaer then embarked on the most frightening week of their lives. They had to act quickly, because news of the merger was beginning to leak to the press.

On Tuesday Doyle Dane Bernbach's stock price shot up $5 a share on rumors of a merger deal. The company suspended trading with the announcement that it was engaged in "business consolidation discussions involving an exchange of securities." On the previous day, April 21, 1986, the last reported sale price of DDB's common stock had been $23.25, not much above its low for the year. On Wednesday morning, the financial press linked Needham's name with the negotiations.

Before the news hit the West Coast, Rubin called two of the men who were his key contacts on the Honda account, waking them up to arrange a meeting as soon as possible. At an oceanside restaurant in Redondo Beach, the two explained what was to occur at the board meeting. "If the merger is agreed to, Honda would be a free agent," Rubin explained.

But instead of being troubled by the development and saying they would begin looking at other large agencies to handle their business, the all-important Honda clients gave their agency partners their support, and Rubin Postaer & Associates was on its way.

Immediately after the breakfast, and breathing a little easier, Postaer and Rubin boarded a plane for their hometown of Chicago to make the 7:00 o'clock board meeting. They were among the minority of the thirteen board members who knew the meeting's true purpose. Reinhard's team of secretaries, however, had to reach all of the board members to tell them the meeting was postponed until 10:00, and further delays pushed the start back until close to midnight.

Meanwhile in New York, feverish preparations were already being made to announce the three-way deal with a press conference following the close of the stock market on the afternoon of Friday, April 25. Press releases were being written, a big meeting room in the Helmsley Palace was reserved, refreshments had been ordered, and lists of invitees were drawn up for last-minute calls.

With squawk boxes linking those assembled in the Chicago high-rise hotel with board members in other countries who were unable to attend, Reinhard launched his polished presentation of the three-way merger, calling the plan a "thrilling new concept."

As he explained it to the board, Needham had few alternatives. Admitting the troubled nature of the New York operation, Reinhard said Needham could either retreat to Chicago and play up its strengths there or continue to try to compete in New York and internationally, all the while being encircled by bigger public agencies with the ability to raise cash for expansion through acquisition. Either way, Reinhard told his colleagues in an impassioned speech, the value of the company would go down. The alternatives were to participate in this merger now, with DDB and BBDO paying a premium for the privately held firm, or to face an uncertain future. But a merger at some point, Reinhard insisted, was inevitable.

It was clear to all of the board members that Reinhard, who owned 10.23 percent of the agency's common stock and 15.5 percent of the preferred shares, considered the merger to be a done deal. Of the 24 million shares to be created in the new holding company, Reinhard explained, Needham shareholders would received 2.9 common shares for each Needham common share and .5 common shares in the new company for each preferred share.

There was resistance to Reinhard's carefully crafted plan, especially from the Chicago-based management team lead by C. A. "Al" Wolfe and creative executive Joel Hochberg. They were disturbed about converting Needham to public ownership and the problem of an agency so strong in Chicago—Anheuser-Busch alone represented 11 percent of the agency's revenues—being managed from New York.

But the members of Needham's board, all major shareholders in the company, would end up with considerable stakes in the newly formed holding company. Reinhard would emerge as the largest single shareholder, with other Needham executives, including Al Wolfe and Richard H. Needham, close behind.

"Money colored the whole thing," one of the board members said later. Needham's board voted to unite with Doyle Dane Bernbach to form a new agency headed by Reinhard.

The nervous and exhausted Los Angeles team declared themselves independent from the merger and took the first morning plane back to Los Angeles to resolicit the rest of their accounts.

BBDO's board meeting, convening on the same evening at 8:00 in the company's old 383 Madison Avenue headquarters, was interrupted by a bomb scare that was phoned in to the building's security department. The executives were forced to evacuate from the eighth floor to another location while the New York Police Department's bomb squad and two BBDO executives not involved in the meeting searched the corporate floor for explosives that never materialized.

BBDO shareholders, according to the agreement, would receive 1.23 shares of stock in the new holding company for each of their BBDO shares, which on the day before the announcement were trading for $33.75.

Schalk and Rosenshine were beginning to sweat about word of the proposed deal leaking out. Schalk contended that the success of the merger negotiations depended on the secrecy of BBDO's involvement. For by this time the BBDO team knew that Saatchi & Saatchi was ready to put on the table at DDB's board meeting a $30-per-share offer to buy the agency with some cash upfront and a payout contingency plan patterned after those it had used to buy Backer & Spielvogel, Dancer Fitzgerald Sample, and many other shops.

"If the Saatchis find out what they're up against they'll beat us to death," Schalk thought.

The Doyle Dane Bernbach board also met on Thursday but disbanded without a firm decision. On Friday, the DDB executives convened again, this time with the firm proposal from BBDO and Needham for the three-way deal.

Austrian and Pfundstein forcefully communicated their negative feelings about the Saatchi organization, and again the arrogance of the Saatchi brothers came into play. They stayed in London, leaving even last-minute dealings to Anthony Simonds-Gooding and their financial men. Additionally, their contingency payout scheme, with which they had coerced other agencies into mergers, was not attractive to the Doyle Dane Bernbach board. The Saatchi offer was rejected.

The board members made the historic decision to join DDB with Needham Harper, effectively ending its existence as an independent agency. "Because of the almost totally unconditional nature" of the BBDO/Needham plan, the board of directors approved the merger, according to the financial documents in the deal. In return for its famous name, its clients, and its people, DDB would trade each of its shares for one share of stock in the new company.

The lengthy discussion at the DDB meeting delayed the planned announcement of the historic three-way merger. By 8:00 on Friday evening, the three agencies had agreed to the deal by telephone, and the lawyers took off to their offices to write the contracts.

The executives gathered at two in the morning on Saturday, April 26, at the offices of the law firm Rogers & Wells in the Pan Am Building to sign the contracts.

"I had just enough time to pick up clean shirts and catch the Concorde to London," Schalk says.

The architects of what would come to be called Omnicom now faced the toughest task of all: informing their clients and their 10,000 staff members around the world of their life-altering decision.

CHAPTER 12

Maurice and Charles Saatchi
were enraged at having lost the bid for Doyle Dane Bernbach
and grew even more furious on Sunday, April 27, when Allen
Rosenshine telephoned Maurice in London to inform him that
it was an unprecedented three-way deal that defeated them.

Rosenshine disclosed that the new holding company, with
$5 billion in billings, had instantly usurped the number-one
position in the advertising industry from Interpublic, which had
$4.7 billion in billings. The dream of Maurice and Charles,
whose recent acquisition spree had boosted Saatchi & Saatchi Co.
billings over $4 billion, was slipping away.

News of what the Omnicom Group architects called the
"Big Bang" was met with reactions ranging from exultant to
neutral. All weekend, from a war room at BBDO headquarters,
the team led by Rosenshine charted the progress of calls made
to clients by executives from all three agencies. Reinhard, Bernbach, and Loughrane, by merging two agencies into one, had
the most explaining to do, especially because Loughrane would
no longer be involved in DDB Needham management. Reinhard
was the new chief executive officer, and Bernbach would rule
the international operation, while Loughrane was to be the chief
executive of a third company in the structure called Diversified

Agency Services. All of the subsidiary companies—public relations firms, sales promotion agencies, health care shops, and smaller regional shops—of the three major agencies would fall into this new group. John Bernbach was in Europe with Willi Schalk, holding their own press conferences and meeting with clients to get the merger underway on the Continent.

A tremendously effective public relations effort on the part of the Omnicom task force thrust the "global creative superpower" into the news in the mainstream media in an unprecedented fashion. Rosenshine, Reinhard, BBDO's new chief executive officer Norman Campbell, and their colleagues were spotlighted not only in all of the country's business magazines but also in a color spread in *Time. Advertising Age,* the industry's leading weekly, lavished praise on the leaders of the biggest advertising company in the world for putting creativity first in forming their new company.

All of this just served to inflame further the proud Saatchi brothers. And to provide Bob Jacoby with the opportunity to get what he had avariciously craved for years—$500 million in cash for Ted Bates Worldwide, the agency he controlled.

John Hoyne returned to Ted Bates in 1982 after spending several years away from adland. When he ran the international division during most of the 1970s, his wife Eugenia and their eight children rarely saw him because much of his time was spent gallivanting with the notorious carouser Jacoby to far-flung capitals where Bates had offices. To preserve his family, Hoyne returned to his native California and operated a lumber and hardware business in Santa Barbara that was less than successful. His enforced separation from the power and fast-lane life-style had served its desired purpose, and Hoyne asked Jacoby to find a place for him.

So Jacoby pushed out Stephen Rose, who had succeeded Hoyne as president of the international division, giving him a job as head of the Bates affiliates group in the U.S., and restored his traveling buddy to his old post. Additionally, Jacoby gave Hoyne responsibility for corporate strategic planning. It was Hoyne's job to work with Jacoby to determine the company's financial future.

Hoyne hired the giant accounting firm Arthur Andersen & Co., at a fee of several hundred thousand dollars, to develop a plan to refinance the agency. Bates was posting profit margins much higher than the industry average, thanks to wise investments in real estate as much as profitability of agency operations. The privately held company's share price was escalating quickly, and the top executives knew it would not be easy to recycle their shares. As the biggest shareholder, Jacoby wanted to maximize the value of his stock and develop a plan so that he and his top managers could cash in. They had no intention of sharing the wealth at retirement with a generation of successors, as did their predecessors who had given them control of the company. Selling Ted Bates for top dollar became Jacoby's number-one priority.

The obvious alternatives presented to the Bates board by Arthur Andersen were long-term borrowing through which Bates could repurchase the big chunks of stock and also finance acquisitions; going public, which was not satisfactory because of limitations on how quickly shares could be sold; and a third option—selling the agency outright.

The consultants determined that within five years profits would be such that, selling at the norm of twelve to fourteen times the earnings, the price should be $500 million. And henceforth, reaping $500 million in cash for Ted Bates became Jacoby's obsession.

Although Hoyne's base of operations was New York, he spent much of his time in the Bates London office. So he was well acquainted with the Saatchis and their plans for worldwide domination of the advertising and communications industry. By the beginning of 1985, the Saatchis had discussed mergers with most of the chief executive officers of independent ad agencies in America, but their representatives had not yet approached Ted Bates. Eased by an initial contact made in London, Hoyne approached the brothers' associate Simon Mellor, and in January they had their first meeting in New York using the Helmsley Palace as their headquarters.

The representatives of the two companies were able to keep the extreme contrasts in their personal styles under cover at the initial meeting. Mellor was close to Maurice, and had taken over the duties of Charles in the early days—creating the agency's public image by artfully managing contacts with the press and wooing analysts in the financial community. He was a few years younger than Maurice, and his reedy build, dark hair, large brown eyes, and delicate movements projected an almost effeminate manner. But the savvy Mellor was emerging as a corporate strategist, and after having first discussed the possibility of selling off only the William Esty Co., he made it clear that it was all of Bates that piqued the interest of the Saatchis, who needed to add power in Asia and Australia where Bates was thriving.

By March, Hoyne thought it was time the principals in the deal met face-to-face and arranged another Helmsley Palace rendezvous. Maurice Saatchi traveled to New York with Simon Mellor.

The Bates side of the table in the conference room of the overly gilded "Palace," as Hoyne called it, represented the older generation: Hoyne, with his silver hair and very masculine style; Jacoby, whose gruff and dated manner of speaking complemented his ever-present cigar; and the Bates financial advisor Ned Pugh, the retired former chief financial officer of Avon Inc., whom Hoyne had retained as a consultant.

The session resulted in an offer from the Saatchi team: $280 million in cash, and the rest according to the normal Saatchi payback plan, a system that could come close to doubling the original sum, over a five-year period, based on the acquired agency's profitability.

Hoyne was the messenger who brought back Jacoby's message that the offer wasn't strong enough.

Once the idea of selling the agency infiltrated Jacoby's mind, his attention to matters involving the agency or its clients was minimal. According to the company's other top managers, the same could be said of Hoyne, who as president of the international division was charged with keeping multinational clients, such as the powerful Mars company, happy, as well as pulling together the diverse elements that ran the company's offices around the world. Even Jacoby realized that Hoyne was not succeeding in handling both of his responsibilities. From his hotel in Sydney, Australia, Jacoby dashed off a note to his New York president, Donald Zuckert, complaining about Hoyne's performance and asking him to consider taking over the international presidency, an offer Zuckert, the agency's second-largest shareholder, declined for family-related reasons.

Because Hoyne wasn't getting the high-ticket offers he and his boss expected, they decided to talk to First Boston Corp. about what steps they should take. Although they did not give First Boston the assignment to shop the company around, word soon began circulating around Wall Street that Bates was on the market. Offers came in from at least five investment groups, all of whom were interested in helping management refinance the company by paying for a piece of the action. But Jacoby and his man Hoyne kept their goal in mind: sell it all and sell it for cash.

Meanwhile, Martin Sorrell, who had masterminded the Saatchi acquisition strategy from 1977 until mid-1985, decided it was time for him to stop enriching the Saatchis, where he would never penetrate the true inner circle, and go off on his own. Just turning 40 years old, Sorrell had built up a great deal of credibility in the London financial community, along with the contacts and resources to start to build a communications and marketing services company of his own. Sorrell put up $600,000 and bought a publicly traded company called Wire & Plastic Products, which manufactured wire shopping baskets, and began to extricate himself from the operations of Saatchi & Saatchi Co.

Sorrell's formula of acquiring firms for a relatively low initial sum and making the future payments out of what were essentially the acquired firm's own profits, had been key to the popularity of Saatchi & Saatchi Co. stock on the London exchange. With Sorrell out of the picture, Hoyne continued his discussions with Simon Mellor. The two met often when Hoyne found himself in London. Hoyne continually made the point that there was no way they could do business unless the Bates shareholders got the cash upfront. "We were not going to take any risk in terms of being paid," Hoyne says.

Jacoby and Hoyne also wanted to be free of any performance obligation to the parent once the deal was done. In all of the other Saatchi deals involving long-term payouts, top managers were tied to five-year contracts that, in the minds of the Saatchis and the eyes of the powers-that-be in the London financial markets, would ensure the future success of the agencies. Continuity in agency management and the maintenance of personal relationships with clients had always been the foundation of a successful agency business. The idea of signing employment contracts was not a problem to Hoyne and Jacoby because it would guarantee that they would continue to be paid. But they did not want to be responsible for profits under a system they knew they would no longer control.

Despite what the Saatchi image-makers—public relations people who would put out puffy statements and never be available to answer questions from the press—said for the record about separate autonomous agencies under their holding company system, it was never Saatchi & Saatchi's intention to honor those commitments.

The advertising community is a small one, especially in New York, and the word was out on the Saatchi modus operandi, largely the invention of Martin Sorrell. Their team of financial people infiltrated a company immediately after an acquisition and performed minutely detailed audits of every phase of operation. The contracts the Saatchis had with the agencies they acquired prohibited the subsidiaries from making their own acquisitions, borrowing funds, giving raises to employees earning more than $100,000, selling assets, and other related transactions, without the approval of Saatchi management.

Autonomy in the world of Saatchi & Saatchi was simply a facade to appease clients. For what Charles Saatchi really wanted, according to his confidants, was to be in such a powerful position, to have such a commanding market share lead in the advertising industry, that he could merge all of his agencies together into one—called simply Saatchi & Saatchi. His clients, he believed, would have no choice but to accept the existence of competing companies, their archrivals in business, being served by Saatchi & Saatchi because there would be scarcely anywhere else to turn.

By early December of 1985, Hoyne and Mellor had reached agreement on many points of negotiations, and Maurice Saatchi began turning up the heat to sign a deal before the end of the year. The British economy was at a stage when many major companies were restructuring financially, and Maurice had to "get in line at the Bank of England," he said, to get financing. Maurice placed a telephone call to Jacoby, one of the few times the two had spoken directly, urging him to bring the deal to a conclusion. Again, the money Maurice was offering fell below that which Jacoby intended to get for his company, and the shrewd New Yorker was prepared to wait it out.

Within a few weeks, Maurice, apparently afraid he would

lose the opportunity to double the company's size, told his negotiators he was ready to make the final push. Saatchi representatives told Hoyne to have the contracts drawn up and come to London to close the deal. The Bates law firm of Cahill Gordon & Reindel quickly prepared the documents stating that Saatchi & Saatchi would pay Bates shareholders $400 million cash initially, to be followed a year later by another payment for a separate class of stock.

On January 9, 1986, Hoyne and Jacoby were scheduled to meet the Saatchi acquisition team in London. The session was set for three in the afternoon at the upper-crust Claridges hotel on Brooks Street.

According to one of the participants in the meeting, "it was a typically English uncomfortable situation." Jacoby and Hoyne were directed to chairs at opposite ends of the table, while Maurice Saatchi, Simon Mellor, and Andrew Woods, corporate finance director, sat between them. Even at this advanced stage of the negotiations, Charles Saatchi did not appear.

Rather than dealing with the contracts, as they had promised, the Saatchi team began negotiating right away. Hoyne interrupted and said directly to Jacoby, "What do you think?"

"I think we should go to the bar," Jacoby replied.

In the lounge, the miffed CEO took a hotel card and wrote on the back: "Simple deal. $500 million cash. No contingencies. No problems." Hoyne and Jacoby felt that Maurice Saatchi was being led around by his financial man and that they had to make their appeal directly to Maurice.

Hoyne returned to the meeting room and gave it another shot. The Bates executives had come over in good faith, Hoyne told them, ready to sign what had been agreed to and not expecting further haggling. Perhaps Bates was too rich for the Saatchi resources, he suggested.

Certainly not, Maurice replied, adding that he was eager to complete the transaction.

Hoyne said the Bates attorney had been called to London. So the meeting concluded at five o'clock, with the parties agreeing to meet again at eleven the next morning.

The negotiations opened the next morning with the Saatchi side putting forth another offer approaching $450 million with the final payment dependent on several contingencies. Hoyne and Jacoby realized that it was "quite a lot of dough," but they were unwilling to argue what they felt were a lot of small points. Andrew Woods, a plain man with gold-rimmed glasses, a receding hairline, and given to tightly fitting double-breasted suits, was taking an antagonistic point of view during the session, which offended Jacoby. The Bates chairman, unlike other agency leaders with whom the Saatchis had dealt, was not overwhelmed by the sums being tossed around. He would not be swayed from the unconditional sum of $500 million he had promised himself. Jacoby rose from his seat at the end of the table and excused himself from the meeting room. Hoyne followed close behind.

"Go up there and tell them to go fuck themselves and don't forget to bring my coat," Jacoby said to Hoyne in the hotel bar.

When Hoyne returned to the assembled group alone, Maurice Saatchi looked perturbed. Was Jacoby coming back, he wanted to know. No, Hoyne told him. Jacoby's gone back to the hotel. We want $500 million, and we want it assured, he explained. This just isn't going to work.

The atmosphere in the room was thick, and both sides believed that was the end of the Bates-Saatchi merger deal.

Hoyne joined Jacoby at his hotel, and they called Bruce McLaren, the London-based president of Ted Bates Europe, to join them for a lavish lunch. Then Hoyne and Jacoby flew back to New York and realized they had to start all over again.

At the Bates annual meeting of top management held in Hawaii that March, Jacoby announced his intention to sell the company and his hope of doing it soon. One factor that he believed would hurt the marketability of the agency was the trouble it was having on its $100 million Colgate-Palmolive account. Jacoby admitted to his managers that he didn't get along with Reuben Mark, the brilliant chief executive officer of Colgate. He knew the account was in "long-term jeopardy," he said, because Colgate recently had pulled some of its European business from Bates and given it to Young & Rubicam.

Jacoby in January had hired John H. Nichols as an executive vice president of the corporation, an adman who had gone through a series of jobs over the past decade, beginning at the Chicago agency Leo Burnett Co. Burnett was a major agency of Procter & Gamble, and Nichols had worked on the account there. He had left to join the Adolph Coors Co. in Golden, Colorado, as a marketing executive, but that tenure was short-lived. Next Nichols tried running a Coors distributorship in northern Tennessee, one of the biggest in the country. Nichols told his associates that he knew how to market beer better than the Coors people, and that he would use his own methods rather than abide by their system. Within eleven months the distributorship was bankrupt. When Nichols was retained by Jacoby, he had promised that his contacts at companies like P&G and Coors would help bring in new business to Bates, both in the U.S. and internationally.

Demonstrating how out of touch he had grown with the workings of the modern advertising world, Jacoby said he thought it would be a good idea to try to persuade John Smale, chairman of Procter & Gamble, to assign Bates $100 million in advertising business, and he would resign Colgate. Young & Rubicam, a few years earlier, had done the reverse. Colgate was promising to make it a major multinational agency for its products, so Y&R's chairman Ed Ney decided, in an unprecedented move thought to be very cheeky, to drop Procter. If Ney could do it, why not Jacoby?

Smale had been the brand manager on Gleem toothpaste decades ago when Jacoby was a young account executive at Compton Advertising. The Bates CEO believed that the connection would help him in 1986, but he was sorely mistaken. The advertising shots at Procter & Gamble were called not by Smale but by one of his key executives, Robert Goldstein. As vice-president of advertising for the country's biggest consumer-products marketer, Goldstein commanded an advertising and promotion budget of $1.6 billion and was a well-respected and tough spokesman for the industry. Jacoby's overtures to Smale proved fruitless, and the situation with Colgate-Palmolive did not improve.

On April 28, Jacoby read the news of the deal that would form Omnicom Group, the biggest agency network in the world. He got his right-hand man Hoyne on the telephone. "Write them a one-page letter and say 'This is what we want. Sign it or not.' " Jacoby correctly read the Saatchis' desperate desire to become number one and their willingness to do anything to achieve that position. He knew their cash hoard was ready to be spent. It was now or never if he was to get his $500 million.

Days later, Hoyne, Simon Mellor, and Maurice Saatchi were together during a lunch of sandwiches in the Saatchi London headquarters. The Saatchi team knew that $450 million was a price the London financial community would be able to accept for an agency that had $329.9 million in revenues for fiscal 1986, an 11.6 percent increase over the previous year. Operating profit was $64.5 million, with additional profits of $10.3 million coming from the sale of real esate.

The Saatchis were insisting on an initial sum of $400 million, with $50 million to come in 1988. Hoyne could not reach Jacoby to get his comment, so he flew to New York to confer with him in person. Together in Jacoby's office they telephoned London. Jacoby had a plan. "Look, Maurice, let's just make it easy," he said. Bates would borrow $57 million from the bank and it would be part of the sum payable to shareholders, and after the acquisition Saatchi & Saatchi would assume the loan. Another $7 million would come from the 120,000 options shares, which were owned by those with the rank of executive vice president and above. They exercised their options at the time of the sale. It would look like $450 million. But Bates shareholders eventually would reap $507 million.

"Well, send all your monkeys over. We'll do it here this time," Jacoby says he told Maurice Saatchi.

At the same time, Hoyne and Jacoby were negotiating with Interpublic Group of Companies chairman Philip H. Geier, Jr., and chief financial officer Eugene P. Beard. "I had more confidence in Geier," Jacoby says, "and I would have preferred to go American, frankly." The Interpublic team agreed to the price, but they didn't have the cash. The Bates and Interpublic executives went together to Morgan Guaranty bank on Fifth Avenue, which was the Bates bank, too, to arrange for financing. The bank officers were reluctant to provide the cash, and Jacoby turned down their alternative financing plans. On May 11, Geier did get the okay for the cash, but by that time it was too late.

On Thursday, May 8, Jacoby, Hoyne, and the Bates lawyers waited for the Saatchi team at the arranged hour of three o'clock. The hours ticked by—five o'clock, six o'clock. If they don't come by seven-thirty, Jacoby said, I'm going home.

Andrew Woods arrived and signed the contracts for the Saatchis. After two weeks the as-yet unnamed Omnicom Group was dethroned as the world's biggest advertising company. Saatchi & Saatchi bought Ted Bates and its $3.1 billion in worldwide billings to leapfrog over Young & Rubicam, JWT Group, Interpublic, and Omnicom to claim the top spot, with $7.5 billion in billings.

In their haste to achieve dominance, the Saatchis failed to investigate the condition of the agency they were buying. They did not weigh client reaction, never plotted a "worst case scenario" in terms of client defections, and were ignorant of the management turbulence that Jacoby had fostered for years.

The Saatchis' unrelenting ambition would bring them losses in terms of clients, money, people, and prestige that they had never imagined.

CHAPTER 13

The Saatchis broke their word with the executives of their newest possession within hours of signing the merger deal.

Jacoby, Hoyne, and Andrew Woods had agreed at their final session that the announcement of the union would be made in Manhattan on Monday morning, to give the Bates team time to make contact with their clients and explain the new relationship. Among the giant companies on the Bates client roster, including Colgate-Palmolive, R. J. Reynolds tobacco company, General Mills, and Warner-Lambert, there were many whose top management and marketing executives would be legitimately concerned about the marriage.

Saatchi & Saatchi, within its quickly growing stable of agencies, had major clients that competed in the marketplace with each of these consumer-products marketers. None of the Bates officials had taken a single step to test clients' reactions to the merger deal in advance. This was not a case of "perceived conflict" but direct competition in many instances. Colgate-Palmolive, for example, a company for which Bates created millions of dollars of television commercials each year, vied for consumers' dollars with many Procter & Gamble brands at Saatchi & Saatchi Compton. Now the profits from the advertising written, produced, and placed in the media for both of these brands, and many other rivals, would be going directly into the coffers of London-based Saatchi & Saatchi Co. And many clients would not be pleased.

Beginning on Friday, May 9, the lovely and capable communications vice-president for Ted Bates, Gina Greer-Whitley, set up round-the-clock telex capabilities at the agency's Times Square headquarters to get the word out to the agency's 102 offices in 44 countries and to prompt the executives abroad to notify their clients. Greer-Whitley and her team also monitored responses from the field, alerting John Hoyne of any major problems. Jacoby was noticeably absent.

As the Bates public relations staff was busily writing press releases to hand out at Monday's news conference, Saatchi & Saatchi was secretly leaking the news to selected reporters in New York and London.

Greer-Whitley called Anne S. McBride, the Saatchis' New York-based press liaison, at her country home on Saturday morning for approval of the Bates press materials. Greer-Whitley wanted to include a quotation from Maurice Saatchi in the release. "The brothers are never quoted," McBride said in her shrill, imperious voice.

A former securities analyst, McBride's post as senior vice-president in charge of romancing the financial community and manipulating the Saatchis' image in the press gave her a sense of power. McBride often turned out for the office in flashy diamond jewelry and a mink coat.

The story leaked into many newspapers on Friday morning, although estimates of the price the Saatchis paid, based on what securities analysts thought would be a fair sum, were far below the actual $507 million.

The Saatchi & Saatchi version of the story, stating that they would pay a total of $450 million, broke in London newspapers Monday morning, as well as in the *Wall Street Journal*, the *New*

York Times, and the advertising trades. At the New York press conference, the Bates team was met by a snarling group of reporters who had been slighted by the Saatchi & Saatchi press agents.

Some of Bates's biggest clients also heard the news second-hand, including Melvin R. Goodes, president of Warner-Lambert. Goodes did nothing to hide his fury at Jacoby's widely reported personal profit of $112 million, nor at being put in a second-fiddle situation to Procter & Gamble without being consulted and without having a chance to prepare for an alternative agency. Goodes was attending the Proprietary Association convention, a conclave of top executives in the nonprescription medicine business at the Greenbrier resort in West Virginia, when the news broke. When the drug-company executives left a few days later, the Greenbrier would be the scene of the American Association of Advertising Agencies annual meeting at which Bob Jacoby would be anointed as the elected chairman for the year.

"Goodes was so mad he could hardly swallow his food," said one of his friends after the meeting.

The combination of the Saatchis' mishandling of the announcement and the arrogance of Jacoby and Hoyne in not testing the waters with clients beforehand brought a swift and furious reaction.

Within two weeks, Colgate-Palmolive chairman Reuben Mark aligned the $100 million in billings that had been at Ted Bates with two agencies he described as "true partners"—Young & Rubicam and Foote, Cone and Belding. Industry watchers and Jacoby's competitors expected him to do the proper and ethical thing when he signed the Saatchi deal—resign the Colgate business. Procter & Gamble, whose dominating presence in the Saatchi world dictated the situation, had a very strict conflict policy of which its agencies were all aware. Direct competition of brands within the same agency family simply was out of the question. But Jacoby did not honorably resign the business; he waited to be fired.

Bates lost Colgate business not only in the U.S. but also in Canada, Mexico, and the Asia-Pacific region, which involved seven countries. All lost major chunks of business ranging from toothpastes to dishwashing liquids to shaving creams.

Colgate's move was the beginning of a client-generated explosion. Executives of major package-goods marketers were quoted in the press as saying the megamerger trend made them feel slighted. "The client is an afterthought and is getting lost in the shuffle. We want an agency who really wants our business, who would kill to get our business," one advertiser said.

The attitude being projected by the Saatchis and Bates management was that the expansion of the Saatchi system and the personal enrichment of Bates executives was infinitely more important than the close business and personal relationships that had been a tradition in the advertising business.

The influential Robert Goldstein of Procter & Gamble made his thoughts on the issue of agency consolidations and client conflicts clear in an interview with *Advertising Age* just weeks after the two biggest mergers in advertising history.

> It's not clear to me why two or three agencies operating with one ownership as parallel networks will contribute anything either to clients or the public, which those same agencies operating separately would not contribute.
>
> In essence, when an agency creates separate networks and argues that these will be kept totally separate, there will be no communications, there will be no transfer of personnel or knowledge, they are making a public statement that they are not looking to gather economies of scale or size.
>
> They are basically saying that the companies we own are bigger, but the parts aren't going to work together.
>
> If the parts aren't going to work together, how can the

clients be served? How can the public be served? How can anybody be served? Those are questions I have not heard an answer to yet.

Just prior to the Bates acquisition, the New York office had been engaged in a battle to keep the Michelob beer account from Anheuser-Busch, a $38 million account. The advertising from Bates was not working to sell beer, and the brand's sales were declining. The Chicago office of Needham Harper, now DDB Needham, prevailed in the competition, and Michelob walked out the door, too, although that loss was not directly related to the merger deal.

The publicity surrounding the Bates sale—especially the unrestrained babbling regarding the astounding cash sums pocketed by its executives—backfired on Omnicom Group, the agency that was the biggest for only two weeks.

"Pre-Saatchi," says Allen Rosenshine, "the reaction to our merger was 'WOW!' Post-Saatchi, we got mired down in the negativism."

Because of the Bates price and all the talk about money, Rosenshine explains, "We thought the comparison would do us good. But there was so much mud flying . . . it brought us under scrutiny, too."

Chief executive officers of publicly held advertising agencies spend much of their time before the financial community persuading analysts and potential investors that advertising really is a stable business, and account shifting and volatility is much less of a factor than one would be led to believe. The summer of 1986 shattered that argument and put the agency community into a demoralizing tailspin. Each day the newspapers reported account losses at the newly merged agencies, and staffers worried about when the axe would fall on them.

Jacoby and his new owners knew they would lose Colgate and expected also the loss of the low-billing General Foods coffee brands Maxim and Mellow Roast (also because of conflicts with Procter & Gamble products). And they were resigned to the fact that Needham had the edge on Michelob. But when Jacoby was giving the Saatchis assurances of his strong ties with clients, Warner-Lambert was offered as the model of stability. The New Jersey company was one of Bates's oldest clients, having been with the agency for thirty years. With $68 million in billings, Bates had turned its Unique Selling Proposition on Warner-Lambert brands to create some of the most unappealing commercials on the air—epitomized by the remedy for relief of heartburn: "R-O-L-A-I-D-S."

The last week in June, Bob Jacoby was honored by the B'nai B'rith in Manhattan as its advertising man of the year, and Warner-Lambert chairman and chief executive officer Joseph D. Williams was one of the speakers. He joked that Warner-Lambert owed the American people an apology for the campaigns Bates had created for its products over the years. Had Warner-Lambert known that Jacoby's agency would come up with slogans so insulting to people's intelligence, the company never would have launched the products, he said.

Just six weeks after Bates was bought, Warner-Lambert president Goodes walked into Jacoby's office and fired him. Goodes reassigned the $68 million in billings to J. Walter Thompson Co., which won Hall's cough tablets, Listermint, and Trident and Bubblicious gums. Young & Rubicam took on the proprietary brands Rolaids, Efferdent, Remegel, and Mediquell.

Jacoby still believes that the agency, "got fired by Warner-Lambert because of ego. Those guys couldn't stand to see the agency getting all that dough."

In the midst of all this bad fortune, Bates, on the strength of creative presentations headed by Ralph Rydholm, won the Xerox Corp. account, which, with $40 million in billings, made up for the loss of Michelob.

The William Esty subsidiary of Ted Bates was the next

agency to be hit by client reaction to the megamerger, as its giant client RJR Nabisco yanked $96 million in billings in one swipe. Esty was founded on R. J. Reynolds tobacco business fifty-four years before, but in recent years the relationship was troubled and Jacoby knew it. Esty had been the long-time agency on RJR's major brand Winston, the cigarette that was the best-selling smoke in the country through the 1960s and early 1970s. But Philip Morris and its agency Leo Burnett Co. had the brilliant vision to create a cowboy personality for Marlboro, which ended up riding right over Winston to the top-selling spot. Esty, which never had a reputation for innovative ideas or anything approaching dazzling creative work, was not able to deliver a campaign that tackled the problem of the continuing encroachment of Marlboro on Winston's market share. Esty was "only reacting" to RJR management, not leading them to a solution.

Once Esty's executives sold to Bates, and split $55 million among a few of them, they were even less inclined to take an activist stance with their clients. By 1985, Esty's five-year autonomy agreement with Bates had expired, and Jacoby started playing corporate politics. He publicly disclosed his intention to put one of his top managers—Don Zuckert or Larry Epting—in command at Esty, a strategy that R. J. Reynolds found objectionable. So Jacoby was given a strong signal in mid-1985 when RJR moved Winston, with $60 million in billings, from Esty and awarded it to McCann-Erickson, while at the same time pulling Sterling, a new brand with an introductory budget of $40 million, and giving it to Chicago agency Tatham-Laird & Kudner.

Helping to precipitate the day of reckoning for Esty was the fact that Backer & Spielvogel, now a sister agency, worked for archrival Philip Morris on Parliament and new products. Additionally, one of the flagship accounts of Saatchi's London office was the Silk Cut brand. RJR cut the $50 million Salem account, which left Esty for Foote, Cone & Belding's newly merged New York operation FCB/Leber Katz. The punishment was completed when RJR pulled products under the Nabisco banner, which it had acquired earlier in 1986. Esty lost Milk Bone and Butcher Bone dog biscuits to another Saatchi subsidiary, DFS Dorland, and Nabisco cookies and Premium saltines and Ritz crackers to McCann-Erickson. The $96 million billings loss accounted for about one fourth of Esty's billings.

Looking on from across the Atlantic, the Saatchis witnessed the value of its expensive acquisition shriveling as the major consumer-products companies they coveted as profitable clients pulled more than $350 million in billings within just a few weeks.

Nor did Omnicom emerge unscathed by client reaction to its deal. Besides having to give up the $100 million in billings from the Los Angeles office of Needham, other conflicts were resolved quickly. BBDO had to resign the $20 million Old Milwaukee account from Stroh Brewery Co. in deference to Anheuser-Busch, especially in light of Needham's Michelob win.

Minneapolis flour and cereal giant General Mills, a major client of DDB Needham/Chicago, took an especially hard line on the conflict issue, making it clear to Rosenshine, Reinhard, and BBDO's new chairman Norm Campbell that they would have to sacrifice all competitors within the Omnicom agency networks. To General Mills, the concept of separate autonomous agencies with one system was not valid. Though Quaker Oats Co. cereals were handled by BBDO/ Chicago, which theoretically was separate from its sister agency DDB Needham across the street, the competition between Wheaties and Quaker cereals such as Life was close to the hearts of the General Mills brass. If Omnicom wanted to retain General Mills, it had to do something about the others.

BBDO/Chicago resigned its $20 million in Quaker billings, a tough blow to that office whose only bigger client was Wrigley chewing gum.

The General Mills stridency also affected a Saatchi subsidiary, the Chicago office of Backer & Spielvogel, which had originally been an in-house agency for Quaker. While General Mills was putting the pressure on Maurice Saatchi to resign the Quaker oatmeal, cereal, granola bar, and Gatorade business that made up almost all of the $50 million in billings of the Chicago office, Carl Spielvogel publicly insisted that he had no intention of doing so. The executive group in Chicago, led by Gary Bayer, privately pondered their options and discussed the possibility of buying the agency from the Saatchis, at the same time that Spielvogel continually declaimed that the branch office was not for sale and berated reporters for "fabricating" stories to this effect.

The Quaker situation was an early example of how little control even the highest-ranking officials of a Saatchi-owned agency had after they collected their sale price. Once the Saatchis decided how they would handle a client conflict or an agency consolidation, no amount of haranguing on the part of their agency executives produced the desired result.

Backer & Spielvogel, Chicago, was sold by Saatchi & Saatchi Co. to its local management group, which as an independent agency under the name of Bayer, Bess, Vanderwarker & Flynn continued to handle the Quaker account.

RJR Nabisco relieved what would become DDB Needham, New York, of its $15 million in Fleischmann's and Blue Bonnet margarine billings because those brands competed directly in the marketplace with Kraft's Parkay margarine at Needham's Chicago office. But, ironically, Needham shortly lost all of its Kraft billings when the Chicago company consolidated its business at other agencies.

The New York office of DDB was also affected by a regrouping of International Business Machines advertising responsibilities, which moved $30 million in billings from what would become DDB Needham.

But while Rosenshine, Reinhard, and the others involved

in planning the Omnicom merger had carefully calculated the account losses they would face and therefore encountered few surprises, Jacoby and Hoyne at Bates had paid no attention to the problem and were continually shocked at the hemorrhaging.

Omnicom's losses stopped at the stage necessary to resolve original conflicts, and the member agencies, especially BBDO, were able to regain momentum and win new business, even during the initially difficult period. BBDO, for example, emerged victorious in a hard-fought battle for the $50 million Apple computer account; and DDB Needham, despite setbacks from Kraft and Sears, Roebuck & Co., was able to bounce back and win new business.

As the account-switch tumult grew, more advertisers were ready to come forth with their points of view. "The merger trend in the ad agency business has significantly weakened relationships between the agency and the client," said Joel Weiner, executive vice-president of corporate marketing for Kraft Inc. Weiner made his attack in a talk before the Association of National Advertisers, with Keith Reinhard, who was to be the next speaker, and his new boss, Allen Rosenshine, seated in the front row.

"It is extremely difficult to empathize and consider the agency a true partner [when] the client wakes up to find a competing brand" being serviced by a branch office or a related agency, Weiner said.

"It is an equally wrenching emotional issue to find your agency helping a competitor beat you in a major product category. It is quite difficult to accept a sharing of management and strategic resources working on competing brands."

Weiner, who administers Kraft's $250 million-plus annual advertising budget, wondered aloud about how the agencies would "maintain high levels of creativity and innovation . . . as the senior executives spend more of their energies on managerial and financial matters."

The issue of agency size also came into play because advertisers want to "remain a key account that is a significant part of the agency's livelihood," the unsmiling and erudite Kraft executive said. "Being one of dozens of $50 million accounts [in a giant agency] is not the same as being one of a few."

At the same highly charged conference at the Homestead resort in Hot Springs, Virginia, J. Tylee Wilson, chairman of RJR Nabisco, a $20 billion company with a $1 billion advertising and promotion budget, denounced the mergers for contributing to the "period of uncertainty" in the business.

"Your empires have been built," Wilson said in comments intended for the many agency executives who were present as speakers and guests. "Now it's time to get back to work.

"Having fought competitors all my life, I don't want them on same block, and I certainly don't want them in the same house," he said. "And don't tell me it's OK because they're in a different wing."

The most troubling result of the giant mergers, Wilson said, is "their effect on people, especially because in agencies, people are your assets. The giant combinations have caused dislocation, disaffection, underperformance and just plain fear."

In this climate, Bates and Esty were subject to bad news every week, even before the Saatchis paid their promised ransom. While the Saatchi accountants were combing the books in the pre-closing audit, billings were walking out the door. And to keep profits up to the promised levels, the first wave of massive staff cuts hit the New York advertising community.

Agency executives argued that mergers were not the only reasons for the staff cuts, but that general softness in client spending forced them to pare their employment rolls. Esty cut fifty people immediately after its RJR Nabisco loss. Bates, whose shareholders were celebrating their fortunes, said it was forced to fire sixty staffers, a number that quickly grew to one hundred before the end of the summer. Needham Harper Worldwide, before it actually moved into the Doyle Dane Bernbach offices, trimmed its New York staff by more than fifty and still did not have room for twenty-eight people of the one hundred and seventy-nine remaining at the unified agency. Doyle Dane Bernbach made room for the incoming Needhamites by firing more than thirty from all departments.

The general anxiety bred by the mergers in the summer of 1986 led Keith Reinhard to launch a regular weekly communication designed to quiet some fears. He set up a "merger hotline" to answer questions for the jittery staff. The Omnicom Group established a computerized human resources data bank that identified job openings within the thirty-six agencies of the group.

But while DDB Needham offices outside of New York stabilized quickly because they were largely unaffected by the merger except for the changes in the agency's leadership, bringing together such contrasting companies as the homey Needham and the proud but decaying Doyle Dane Bernbach was a formidable task.

Reinhard tried to counter the nay-sayers in one of his weekly memos with a little quiz. Could agency citizens identify which leader, the late Bill Bernbach or Paul Harper, the chairman emeritus of Needham Harper Worldwide, made each of six statements?

For example, Harper said, "We are in the business of changing things. We, as advertising men and women, are the great energizers of this marketplace. And the force that makes this possible is easily labeled but hard to define. Very simply stated, it is Creative Fire."

"However much we would like advertising to be a science —because life would be simpler that way—the fact is that it is not. It is a subtle, ever-changing art, defying formularization, flowering on freshness and withering on imitation," said Bill Bernbach.

Reinhard offered these and other sentiments as evidence that "we are pretty much alike after all."

But the Bernbach legacy that would prove to be Reinhard's biggest obstacle came to light in the quavering voice of Paula Green, one of Bernbach's early "children," who operates an agency under her own name in a spare office near Manhattan's garment district.

On Thursday, August 28, the shareholders of Doyle Dane Bernbach packed the eighth-floor auditorium of the Time-Life Building on Sixth Avenue, in the presence of founder Maxwell Dane, and voted the once-great company out of existence. Paula Green rose at the conclusion of the meeting and unexpectedly asked the audience to pay tribute to "three great people—Bill Bernbach, Ned Doyle, and Max Dane.

"May the tradition continue even though the name may change," she said to the teary-eyed crowd.

CHAPTER 14

When in a fit of pique Bob Jacoby took his portrait off the foyer wall in the executive suite of the Ted Bates offices, he brought to a climax the internal management battles that he himself had incited for years.

Early during the week of September 15, 1986, the third chairman of Ted Bates Worldwide realized that his reign was over. No longer did he have the absolute power that had altered both this $3.1-billion ad agency and his own personality during the past thirteen years. At age 58, Jacoby had his $112 million in the bank, but now he also had a boss. At least one. Thinking he would comfort one of his biggest clients with a letter stating the agency was autonomous and that he reported only to Maurice Saatchi, Jacoby requested such a letter from London. Jacoby brandished the letter about as proof that he still had authority over Bates, but like many of Saatchi's public statements, the letter had little truth behind it. Jacoby signed away his independence when he sold the company, a fact that he came to grips with only after the Saatchi lieutenants marched in to expel him from the agency less than two months after the sale to Saatchi & Saatchi was completed.

When Jacoby took back all 30,000 of the B shares of the company's stock from other board members in the mid-seventies, for which he paid 50 cents per share, he controlled all of the voting power and thus the board of directors. As part of the deal with the Saatchis, the investment banking house Lazard Frères was called in to appraise the value of the voting shares. Jacoby sold them for $40 million.

He had long before abolished the agency's compensation committee and, despite the urging of the board of directors, had no intention of reestablishing it. Jacoby alone, and in his own handwriting, determined who in the company received bonuses and how much they got. Although department heads made recommendations, the final decision was Jacoby's. No voting, no vetos. For the year 1985–86—Bates's fiscal year ended on March 31—Jacoby paid himself a bonus of $700,000. Sizeable bonuses ranging from $3,000 to $300,000 also went to other executives—in account service, creative, research, and finance departments—with the rank of vice-president or above. The exceptions to the "executive" criterion were Jacoby's secretary, Eileen Drgon, who received a $10,000 bonus that year, and the shapely thirtyish secretary–administrative assistant, Jennifer Van Liew, who had been with the company for only one year and received a bonus of $20,000. Jacoby publicly referred to Van Liew as "a social friend." Jacoby's driver also made the bonus list, pulling in $6,000 from company profits.

The domineering chairman also decided who was allowed to buy stock in the agency, the key carrot for retaining talented and hardworking people prior to Jacoby's decision to sell. The company by-laws said that shareholders had to be vice-presidents, have a salary of $35,000 or more, and be on staff for one year. Many employees met the requirements, but it was Jacoby's call as to who received the opportunity to become wealthy through the company's quickly appreciating book value.

When Jacoby decided to make a management change, the candidate had little choice but to accept the appointment. There was no court of appeals. In 1983, Jacoby needed to name a new president of the New York operation, and he took five executives in contention to Puerto Rico and staged a contest. The five, with Don Zuckert and Jacoby looking on, each gave presentations focusing on different issues of agency strategy in a dark meeting room in the basement of the Dorado Beach hotel.

Zuckert, who worked closely with Jacoby in his corporate post in charge of acquisitions, was approached by his boss at the end of the sojourn and asked to ride next to him on the way home. When the plane took off for New York, Jacoby told his second-in-command that the Puerto Rico conference was a "set-up." "You're taking the job," he told the 49-year-old lawyer-adman.

Zuckert was sputtering mad. He loved his job as the acquisitions maven and had thus far added agencies with close to $1 billion in billings to the Bates fold. All of the deals, with the exception of McDonald & Little in Atlanta, were successful in meeting the corporate plan—buying companies that were strong in their regions, with management staffs in place, that needed little attention or interference from the Ted Bates honchos. Bates just collected the profits.

Jacoby was proposing to take away Zuckert's corporate duties as well as throwing him into the fire of a job that required day-to-day client contact, an area from which the loquacious Zuckert had been removed in recent years. But Zuckert was given an ultimatum. Say yes on Monday, Jacoby told him, or hand in your resignation.

Zuckert took the job, and the figures show he handled it well. Billings in the flagship office grew steadily and the office posted profit margins that were far above the industry average. In addition to new business from Avis Rent A Car and Commodore computers, Zuckert helped to add increased billings from many current clients ranging from Maybelline to Ralston-Purina to Prudential insurance to Warner-Lambert. One of his key executives, Larry Light, contributed much to that profitability.

Light's relationship with Mars Inc. co-chairman Forest Mars helped to build the Mars candy and pet food business at Bates into one of the agency's most lucrative accounts. Mars also entrusted Bates with much of its international business, and Light, an ambitious and unconventional intellectual, was eager to turn his success with Mars into a more powerful position for himself.

As Jacoby's business emphasis moved from agency operations to the company's financial restructuring, and he was also spending more time away from the office socializing, Zuckert and Light started concentrating on planning strategy for the agency's internal growth. They would meet on Sundays at Zuckert's compound on the water in Greenwich, Connecticut, and try to figure out where the company was going and how they could help it get there.

To Jacoby's mind, their working on weekends was evidence of a conspiracy against him. To thwart their efforts, Jacoby brought in John Nichols as an executive vice-president and put him in charge of a drive for new business on a global level. Nichols was not given a staff or a budget, however, which set him up in a battle with Zuckert and international managers such as Bruce McLaren, who were forced to defend their turf and people.

While Nichols himself had at best a checkered career record, he "went around telling everyone that Bates was a piece of shit," said one of the key executives. From his first day on the premises until the Saatchi deal was announced in May, Nichols never brought in one piece of new business.

One of the few contingencies to which Jacoby agreed in the negotiations with Saatchi & Saatchi was to get his key executives to sign employment contracts, binding them for five years to certain titles and responsibilities. Jacoby's contract, as chairman of Ted Bates Worldwide, gave him a salary and perquisites of $1.2 million a year.

Larry Light used the occasion to give Jacoby an ultimatum

of his own. He said he would not sign the contract he had been given that described his duties as primarily focused on the Mars Inc. account. Light wanted to be president of Ted Bates International, as he had repeatedly told Jacoby during the past few years, both in writing and in person. Light's credentials, backed by sixteen years at BBDO, included the coordination of a Harvard Business School study on the subject of strategic thinking in the world marketplace. Jacoby, working late into the evening with his suit coat off and his tie open, tried to threaten him. Anybody who didn't sign that night would have to sell back their shares at book value, about $390. Good-bye to the astounding price the stock would bring with the Saatchi acquisition—$853.02 per share.

But Light was holding the trump card, and now was the time to play it. If Jacoby didn't give him the job he wanted, Light would walk away with the Mars account to another agency, and the Saatchi deal would most likely collapse. Light won the trick.

With Zuckert's help, Light had drawn up a job description for a vice-chairman title that could go to John Hoyne, who would forfeit the international job.

The next day Jacoby went to Hoyne and explained the situation. If Light didn't get the international job, he was going to make life with Mars difficult.

A few weeks after the Saatchi deal was signed, the new appointments were announced, with the angle that Bates was putting more support into its international operation. "The primary reasons behind our sale to Saatchi—increasing client consolidation, greater client expectations for global service and broadening consumer markets worldwide—are the same reasons behind these important promotions," Jacoby said in the announcement. Hoyne's job was positioned as including strategic planning, acquisitions, and administration of worldwide operations.

But during the summer, Jacoby stewed about having been

pushed around by Zuckert and Light. He was angry enough to tell people that "Larry Light blackmailed me into making him president of international."

Just weeks after announcing the new management structure, Jacoby told Hoyne his plan. The day after "payday," he decided, he would write Maurice Saatchi a letter outlining some management changes he wanted to make. He would punish Zuckert and Light and put Hoyne in charge of both of them.

But before zinging his underlings, Jacoby had some last-minute bookkeeping chores to attend to. The chairman had promised stock to a short list of executives at the March 31 closing price of $390 per share. Some of these agreements were part of a contractual obligation in the early 1986 acquisition of Chicago-based direct marketing agency Kobs & Brady. Others were based on employment agreements with senior vice-presidents and executive vice-presidents in the agency. In total, 39,000 shares were granted between the announcement of the merger with Saatchi & Saatchi and the payout date of August 7.

Two of the names on the list of shareholders requested by Saatchi management were not executives in the company. Nor did they have the cash or the borrowing capability to buy the combined 3,500 shares on their own. So on August 6, Jacoby took his two friends to Morgan Guaranty bank and arranged for them to borrow money for one day. Jennifer Van Liew took a loan for $980,775 to cover the 2,500 shares that she would be sold, and Eileen Drgon needed only $392,310 to purchase 1,000 shares. For being Jacoby's social friend, Van Liew was able to turn that loan around and reap net proceeds of $1.9 million on her stock, for the first installment, paying only $1,370.40 interest. Another payment of $219,071.50 would be forthcoming in 1988, per the merger agreement. Drgon more than doubled her money, too, with an interest payment of $548.16.

It did not take long for word of Jacoby's largesse to the ladies to travel through the Bates office, and the outrage was palpable. Not only were there qualified executives who had been denied stock while Jacoby ignored protocol and indulged his friends, but the shares distributed to the two secretaries diluted the profitability to legitimate shareholders. Why couldn't the chairman reward his friends out of his own millions, rather than to flaunt hubristically their relationships at the expense of other employees? everyone grumbled.

Having completed the deal, Jacoby was ready to make his move against the men he believed to be his enemies in New York. Just after the payout, Jacoby posted his letter to Maurice, explaining that he wished to make Hoyne president and chief operating officer of Ted Bates Worldwide. Zuckert, whom the chairman described to his new boss as a "housekeeper," was to be given what he said was a powerless post, that of vice chairman. Jacoby and Hoyne sniggered together that since Zuckert had made up the job for Hoyne, saying it was an important job, he would be in no position to complain. Jacoby asked for a cabled answer so that he could act soon.

But Maurice did not respond to Jacoby's note, and lacking approval, the Bates chief did nothing.

Fueling Jacoby's fury was an international management meeting in London in mid-August, to which Saatchi representatives were invited, that Zuckert and Larry Light attended. As newly installed president of the international system, Light wanted to talk to the managers about his vision of a united global ad agency that could function effectively on multinational accounts. Jacoby, they believed, convinced himself that they were trying to poison the Saatchi team against him and take over management for themselves, a contention Zuckert denies. "I never met Maurice until six weeks after Jacoby was gone," Zuckert says.

Just after Labor Day, Anthony Simonds-Gooding, the chairman of Saatchi & Saatchi Communications, arrived in New York to begin his arduous task of trying to get the management of the Saatchi agencies in America to come to an agreement on the consolidations that the brothers had always envisioned. At ten in the morning on September 3, he met with Jacoby and presented him with several options and combinations involving: a Bates merger with DFS Dorland or Saatchi & Saatchi Compton; the possibility of Backer & Spielvogel joining with Saatchi & Saatchi Compton; or, he proffered, they could put all of the agencies together, as Charles Saatchi really wanted to do—Saatchi & Saatchi Compton, Backer & Spielvogel, DFS, and Bates, all under one management team, which, although Jacoby didn't know it, was supposed to be headed by the well-respected Carl Spielvogel.

Ten minutes before the scheduled noon conclusion of the meeting, Jacoby raised the question of reorganizing Bates management, mentioning to Simonds-Gooding the letter he had sent to London a month before. The appearance and demeanor of Simonds-Gooding, who is about ten years younger than Jacoby, says London as surely as Jacoby's says New Jersey. Born in Dublin, with an English father whose travels took the young Anthony to India, he had been a top executive at the British brewing giant Whitbread's prior to taking over the position of the Saatchis' chief presence in the U.S.

Their position, Simonds-Gooding explained to the over-anxious Jacoby, was simple. Saatchi management felt it was time to pause and catch their breath a bit and to get to know each other better before saying yes to such a change. Additionally, he said, accomplishing some consolidation was a top priority. And Jacoby promised Bates's full cooperation in any consolidation moves. "Whatever you want, we will do our best," Simonds-Gooding remembers him saying.

But regarding the appointments, Simonds-Gooding wanted to know, "Will this go down well? Do these people approve?" And, most important, he asked, Would the appointments get in the way of any merger within the agency networks the Saatchis might have in mind?

Jacoby told Simonds-Gooding that Zuckert "would be delighted" with his new job. "He would be a round peg in a round hole," he said, contending that since Zuckert never wanted the New York presidency in the first place, he would welcome the chance to be released from the job.

Nichols, having been with the agency for only eight months, was one of the team who did not sign a personal service contract with the Saatchis and would be a welcome infusion of new blood in the New York operation and would "freshen everyone up," Jacoby said.

In Light's case, Jacoby told Simonds-Gooding he would just be getting Hoyne as a new boss. Hoyne would be able to handle the financial side of the business, which Jacoby said Light found boring.

In the case of a merger with one of the other Saatchi shops, the problem would be the future of Hoyne, for whom the Saatchis were not planning a top position. But Jacoby said that Hoyne was very faithful and "will do what I ask him."

Based on Jacoby's assurances, Simonds-Gooding agreed.

Immediately after the meeting, Jacoby sat in his office and handwrote the letters that would be his undoing. Without any personal contact with the two people who would be most disturbed with the reorganization, Jacoby made his move. He scribbled a note to Zuckert, informing him of his new title of vice chairman and that Nichols, for whom Zuckert had little respect, would be taking his job. At the same time, he dashed off the memo that would inform the New York office of the changes. Zuckert's letter, Jacoby told his secretary Eileen Drgon, was to be on his desk in the morning, simultaneous with the announcement going to the 700-plus people in the New York office. A new president of the company and a new vice chairman had been put into place with no approval from—nor even a meeting of—the company's board.

Jacoby left New York Wednesday evening with his wife

Monica for a retreat in Colorado, from which they would go to the western region American Association of Advertising Agencies convention in Lake Tahoe. Jacoby was scheduled to deliver his first major speech since he took over the post the previous spring, to much ribbing from the podium and behind the scenes about his giant cash stash and ownership by the British.

Jacoby's speech in Tahoe, written for him at a fee of $15,000 plus expenses by former Leo Burnett Co. executive Carl Hixon, was a good excuse to be incommunicado while chaos ensued in New York.

Zuckert, furious at what Jacoby had done, immediately consulted his lawyer, who told him to inform the Saatchis and Jacoby of his displeasure with the developments that had breached the contract he had signed just months before. Zuckert, on Thursday, also sent a memo to the New York staff, informing them that the morning's announcement "was as much a surprise to me as it was to you."

Despite the fact that Nichols, who was calling his friends around the country to tell them the news, now had his job, Zuckert, on advice of his attorney, continued to report to his office, putting in regular hours and doing little more than reading his horoscope in the newspaper.

Legal papers regarding the breach of contract were filed by Zuckert's lawyer on Friday, September 5, and the Bates lawyers said they would settle the contract. But days went by without any contact between the two parties, and Zuckert continued his routine of sitting in his office, reading newspapers. The middle of the next week, Simonds-Gooding made contact with Zuckert, and the deposed president and his ally Light had a chance to tell the Saatchi executive what they felt was really going on. Jacoby, they believed, was out of control, his judgment clouded by his illusions of absolute power.

Zuckert and Light met several times that week with Simonds-Gooding, who was feverishly trying to work out the agency consolidations at the same time. At a rendezvous at the Hampshire House hotel, Simonds-Gooding experimented with a way to fit Zuckert into his plans for merging Bates with Saatchi & Saatchi Compton. "How would you like to be vice chairman of the board in charge of human resources?" the British executive offered.

Zuckert turned him down flat, and not politely, and the two Bates executives took off for a favorite Italian restaurant in Greenwich and proceeded to get drunk.

It was becoming evident to all of the managers at Saatchi agencies in New York that the Londoners had no firm plan for consolidation that would please both clients and the agencies' executives. Jacoby's abrupt switches at Ted Bates, with its subsequent turmoil, put the agency in an even more vulnerable position as far as clients were concerned. "Clearly we must be the major new business target of every agency in town," Zuckert told the *New York Times.* "On the one hand they're saying this is bad for the industry and then they're giving all these stories to the press about how awful mega-mergers are. I wish Ed Ney [Young & Rubicam chairman] would put us in Y&R's profit sharing plan. We've given them half of their new business this year."

On September 10, Saatchi & Saatchi got a firsthand opinion of what Procter & Gamble thought about its dealings in the United States. Bob Goldstein, Procter & Gamble's vice-president of advertising, said the company was moving about $85 million in billings from Saatchi agencies because of "competitive conflict considerations." P&G, the most reticent of companies, rarely discusses its motivation for any dealings with ad agencies. Goldstein was clearly displeased. Saatchi & Saatchi Compton lost Crisco and Crisco oil and the Duncan Hines baking-mix line, and its subsidiary DFS Dorland relinquished Luvs disposable diapers and Bounty paper towels. The beneficiaries were independent agencies: Grey Advertising, Cunningham & Walsh, and

Leo Burnett Chicago, already P&G shops. Jordan, Manning, Case, Taylor & McGrath, a small New York agency, was given P&G business for the first time.

Maurice and Charles Saatchi were in an untenable situation. In their lust for the number-one spot, they had paid almost twice as much for Bates as Wall Street analysts had predicted. And within months, about 10 percent of the revenue base had walked out the door. Many more major accounts—including the $150 million Nissan Motor Corp. at the William Esty Co. subsidiary, and Bates's Maybelline and Ralston-Purina accounts—were on shaky ground. Forest Mars, a stickler for total agency loyalty, was not shy about expressing his annoyance about pet foods and candy products marketed by competitors being served by Saatchi agencies both in the U.S. and abroad. Bates was at a standstill, wracked by rumor and fear about the future. And its most important client had rendered a public slap in the face.

Larry Light waited until the key moment and played his second trump card. Light had made it clear to his people at the Mars headquarters in McLean, Virginia, that he was most unhappy with the recent turn of events at Ted Bates. Mars was the biggest account that Bates had left, and its loss would render the Saatchi purchase essentially worthless. Forest Mars put in a telephone call to Maurice Saatchi, instructing him to do something to remedy the offense that had been inflicted on Light.

By the weekend, Simonds-Gooding knew he had to get rid of Jacoby. On Monday he offered him a corporate job in Saatchi & Saatchi Communications, helping him to consolidate the networks and in the process eliminate 1,500 jobs worldwide. The job, which Jacoby would never accept, breached his contract, and although the Saatchis would be forced to pay him, they would get him out of the picture. The Saatchi mystique, which had so charmed Jacoby in the previous months, was now working against him. "Those brothers are very devious," Jacoby said.

The little chairman had lost control of the one thing that

had made his existence meaningful. "Bates was my life," Jacoby says. "I destroyed my family. I didn't see those daughters of mine for the first twenty years of their lives."

Jacoby removed his portrait from the twenty-seventh floor, he said, because he knew Bates was going to be merged with another Saatchi agency, moved to the company's new headquarters on Hudson Street, and the agency he built would be no more. He told everyone he was buying the painting, the final work by Bud McNally, to give as a present to one of his daughters. It was last photographed hanging above the fireplace in a staged photograph intended to represent his Saddle River home.

On Friday, September 19, while Jacoby was in Washington at a board meeting of the industry association he headed, the Saatchis appointed Don Zuckert chief executive officer of Ted Bates. Jacoby was informed of his ouster by a reporter from *Advertising Age* who was trying to nab him for an interview. Hoyne and Nichols were out of jobs as well.

"Our businesses have a full degree of operational autonomy and it's only if there's a matter that has an impact on the strategic or financial condition that would warrant our interference," Anne McBride said in her statements to the press. "This could have an impact on both. If the clients aren't happy and the people at the agency aren't happy, it certainly could impact on their earnings."

The financial community started to believe that perhaps the Saatchis really didn't know anything about running ad agencies in the United States, or how to retain important clients, and their stock price dropped from about $37 per share when Bates was acquired to about $26. "What's changed is that [the Saatchis seem] to be leading with their chin, to be providing evidence that their critics have been right all along," said James Dougherty, vice-president of research at Country Securities.

Again, the Saatchis and Bates were faced with the embarrassment of deposed executives refusing to leave the premises. Jacoby, who was never officially fired, persisted in occupying his office, though no one spoke to him, and collecting a salary from the Saatchis. His complaint regarding breach of contract went into a lengthy arbitration battle. Hoyne and Nichols simply disappeared, settling their salary disputes through lawyers.

Clients pressed on with their bailouts from the troubled agency, with General Foods, for example, pulling the rest of its account, $25 million in billings. Bates was left with little of a consumer-products base, and further staff cuts, both at Bates and its Esty subsidiary, followed the account losses.

Maurice Saatchi was forced to swallow his pride and to deal with clients' concerns on the subject of conflicts. While executives of his agencies were still spouting that their agencies had no relationships with other Saatchi agencies and therefore should be able to handle competing accounts, Maurice and Charles knew that their plans called for major consolidations, whether their executives liked it or not. As a result, Saatchi resigned close to $15 million in billings from major clients in Europe—Nestlé and Rowntree Mackintosh—to make peace with Forest Mars. And they worked toward the inevitable result of having to give up Cadbury business at DFS Dorland, also as a result of Mars's discontent.

The realities of the American marketplace were forcing the Saatchis to strip away the duplicity of the public statements made in contrast with their private plans. In the United States, the Saatchis were not the bigger-than-life cultural heroes they had become in London. Giant companies such as Procter & Gamble and Mars, which dwarfed Saatchi & Saatchi, were controlled by men who ruled with their dollars. The Saatchi artifice was crumbling. The emperors had no clothes.

CHAPTER 15

Don Johnston was approaching the age of 60, the milestone at which J. Walter Thompson Co. top executives customarily were obliged to turn over the reins to someone else.

By outward appearances, Johnston had accomplished much during his tenure, expanding JWT beyond the advertising business through acquisitions to build JWT Group. He had served as a distinguished chairman of the American Association of Advertising Agencies, despite the scandal that besmirched his company's reputation that same year. He projected the image of a senior statesman of the industry.

But internally, Johnston was preoccupied with politics. Retaining control of JWT became more important to the steely CEO than was the foundation of the business: creating advertising that works and maintaining strong relationships with clients. In mid-1985, Johnston began to survey seriously the candidates for the role of chairman of the $3 billion advertising agency, and Johnston realized two men avidly craved the job. Burt Manning, the creative chief and chairman of the U.S. company, was in his mid-fifties and viewed the worldwide post as a logical culmination of his career. And there was Wally O'Brien, five years younger than Manning, who, as president and chief operating officer of

JWT/USA, played a key role in saving the New York office from degenerating following the Marie Luisi scandal. Working as a sometimes reluctant team, Manning and O'Brien had boosted billings, profits, and the image of the U.S. company to the point that it was named Agency of the Year by the number-two trade magazine, *Adweek*. Johnston had named O'Brien a vice chairman of the worldwide agency and director of multinational client services. In this post, O'Brien was setting up a system of centralized management for the agency's global accounts, such as Pepsi-Cola, Kodak, Kraft, and IBM. The job gave O'Brien entrée to the chief executives of Thompson's biggest clients around the world, a factor that pointed to his being groomed for the top spot.

There were problems with both of the potential candidates, although Johnston did not let them know he believed so. Manning's unusual personality and rampant egotism could potentially be damaging in the inevitable social situations with clients, especially on a global basis. A sound strategist and advertising problem-solver, he tends to ramble in self-serving platitudes when it comes to discussing broader issues. For a creative leader, Manning's shaggy graying beard and clothing that is clearly expensive but often askew was appropriate, but for an international corporate CEO more finesse is required. O'Brien, who favors custom-tailored three-piece pinstripe suits and a pocket watch, was considered even by his rival Manning to be one of the most accomplished account men in the business. But he was not always trusted by his co-workers, some of whom have described him as being dreadfully ambitious.

Both of these seasoned admen had a legion of supporters and years of top-management experience. They were independent in the ways they pursued their business goals, both on client business and internally. They were, in other words, threatening to Johnston. Because, although Johnston was prepared, at least outwardly, to surrender control of J. Walter Thompson Co.

prior to age 60, he would not, in fact, be relinquishing his power over the biggest subsidiary of the holding company. Johnston would remain chairman of JWT Group, a post that had no customary retirement age because Johnston was the first to occupy it. No matter which executive he installed as his successor of J. Walter Thompson Co., Johnston would still be the boss.

Without ever letting on to either of the two men who so intensely wanted the job, Johnston, in June 1985, approached Joe O'Donnell, who had been running the Chicago office for the past three years, about being chairman of the entire company. Joe was 43, and managing the $500-million Chicago office was the highest-ranking job of his career to date. O'Donnell told Johnston that he would take the job of chief executive officer and chairman-elect (Johnston would not give up the chair until the end of 1986) if all further decisions about the succession would be left to him.

The two executives talked on a monthly basis through the summer and the fall. They met at Johnston's Connecticut home on weekends, planning other elements of the agency's management succession, and in most cases Johnston yielded to the younger executive's wishes. Johnston enjoyed the role of teacher and says he grew close to Joe. O'Donnell voiced his determination to give "the key players"—Manning; John E. Peters, the U.S. company's president and chief operating officer; W. Lee Preschel, president of the Latin American and Central Pacific regions; and Jeremy Bullmore, head of the United Kingdom operation—central roles in the future of the company.

O'Brien did not fit into O'Donnell's vision of where the company was going. The chairman-to-be considered the multinational client-service system O'Brien was engineering to be expensive and unnecessary, despite his own lack of any managerial or even casual experience with the international system.

O'Donnell believed that the most professionally driven systems in the Thompson company were the ones that were the most profitable, namely the Detroit and Chicago offices, which he had previously managed. By professionally driven, O'Donnell meant that the offices created popular, prize-winning ad campaigns, grew incrementally in size, and were able to pay competitively and attract good people to work there.

Although the succession plan was not to be announced until spring of 1986, word that O'Donnell was leaving for New York began leaking out in Chicago as early as the autumn of the previous year. O'Donnell denied the rumors good-naturedly, going so far as to put "not for sale" signs outside the stately house in north suburban Winnetka he shared with his petite wife Barbara and four children. Photos were snapped for distribution to the trade press.

Few observers imagined that O'Donnell would be getting the top job in the worldwide company, but the speculation surrounding Johnston's management succession plan kicked off a preliminary executive purge. The first took place in Chicago, where executive creative director Ralph Rydholm expected to be named as the general manager succeeding O'Donnell. Rydholm, a jovial, hard-working, and hands-on creative man, had many loyal followers, and he believed that his years of client connections and well-respected work—which was being touted by agency management in image-building self-promotions—would guarantee him the post.

But Manning and O'Donnell were looking outside the agency for a new general manager, and when Rydholm became aware of what he believed to be their breach of faith, he let it be known that he was available. Don Zuckert and Bob Jacoby were able to entice him to move to New York to join Bates, with the promise of big bucks and the opportunity to transform the Bates creative product into something the agency could be proud of.

Rydholm left the rarefied atmosphere of JWT for the grittier Bates, and the contrast between his posh office in Chicago's John Hancock Building overlooking Lake Michigan and the Bates

Times Square headquarters made for a winter of culture shock. Rydholm likes to symbolize his feeling by recounting a story of leaving the Bates offices late on a cold winter night and waiting to cross the bustling Broadway intersection. A habituée of the neighborhood, a lady of the evening, approached him and commented that it looked as if he had a rough day. "Yeah," Rydholm said, "but no thanks, I'm really not interested."

"We've both got to get out of this business," the hooker said as she took off for another prospect.

As the date for the announcement of the executive changes grew nearer, Johnston took the next steps to clear the deck for O'Donnell. Early in 1986, O'Brien, in a painful meeting with Don Johnston, received the word that there was no room for him in the reorganization that was to come. It was a heartbreaking blow for the lifelong Thompsonite, who had early in his career set the chairmanship of the agency as his goal. The agency announced the resignation of O'Brien, and the news came as a shock to his friends and clients. At 49, O'Brien's career with the agency he loved was finished by corporate politics, and his future was uncertain.

Weeks later, through a press release, it became clear that Johnston was forsaking another contender for the top job, Burt Manning. On February 19, JWT Group announced that Manning was being nominated to the holding company's board of directors, while retaining his titles of chairman of J. Walter Thompson U.S.A. and vice chairman of J. Walter Thompson Co. He was being handed a consolation prize.

In an interview at the time of the announcement, Johnston said that Manning was not getting the chairmanship of the agency because, at 54, he was too old. Johnston said he had wanted the new chairman to commit to the post for ten years and that Manning was unwilling to do so.

Manning's contrived statement at the time of the announcement did little to hide the political struggle at the top. "If I could invent the ideal job, it would be this one: to work with our U.S. people to maintain our record of success and to make a contribution to the growth of the JWT Group companies as well. I already enjoy an active and productive relationship with the executives who will become the new management of the worldwide J. Walter Thompson Co. Becoming a director of the JWT Group board will allow me to provide a creative/business perspective that will be useful to all of the JWT Group companies."

Six months later, on the morning of August 14, Manning abruptly resigned from JWT after twenty years with the company. The next day he was in his new office at 445 Park Avenue, where his name would go on the door as chairman of the executive committee. A six-year-old agency with billings in the $200 million range would be renamed Jordan, Manning, Case, Taylor & McGrath.

On March 5, following the company's board of directors' meeting, Johnston announced O'Donnell's appointment, along with other changes in the corporate structure. Jack Peters, an old Detroit chum of O'Donnell's, was given the title of president and chief operating officer of the worldwide company, while retaining the same titles in the U.S. company.

Another member of the younger generation, Robert L. Dilenschneider, 42, a Chicago PR man, was taking over the JWT subsidiary Hill & Knowlton as chief executive officer, succeeding Loet Velmans, who would retire.

O'Donnell and Peters knew they were inheriting a giant, well-respected $3 billion agency with over 10,000 employees that was performing under par. Revenues from international operations had been flat since 1982, hovering in the $160 to $170 million range. U.S. revenues increased steadily, up to $250 million in the year before the new team took over. JWT does not publicly disclose net income from its individual operations, but with 1985 revenues of $422 million, out of $582.4 million for the entire group, the worldwide ad agency accounted for more than 70 percent of the company's business. Despite changing conditions in the world of advertising, Johnston was ineffective in cutting company costs. Profit margins continually hovered around 4 percent, while comparably-sized agencies were bringing in 11 to 12 percent.

The agency was caught in the difficult trap that made its executives quietly question the issue of public ownership. As an advertising agency, JWT was eminently successful, providing good service to its clients and projecting a strong industry image, thanks to the creative leadership of Manning and the client-contact skills of Johnston. They fostered an atmosphere of pride in the company despite the fact that JWT had given up its billings lead first to Young & Rubicam in 1980 and then was surpassed by four other companies.

But as Johnston the adman had advanced to become Johnston the corporate leader, he set up a new challenge for himself that for reasons his colleagues believe were emotional ones, he did not meet. By retaining the chairmanship of the ad agency from the 1980 formation of JWT Group until 1986, Johnston never really performed his role as the corporate leader. He maintained his close relationships with the top executives of client companies, including Kellogg, Eastman Kodak, Goodyear Tire & Rubber Co., Chevron in California, and the close-to-his-heart U.S. Marine Corps, because he felt comfortable in this area in which he was a well-respected expert.

When he should have been heeding the advice of financial men on the subject of improving the holding company's earnings, Johnston instead dismissed a series of them, resulting in a turn-over averaging close to one chief financial officer per year. While he could have borrowed a strategy from the operators of public agencies such as Foote, Cone & Belding Communications and especially Saatchi & Saatchi Co.—romancing the financial analysts who make recommendations on the company's stock—Johnston instead dealt with them curtly, refusing to disclose his supposed plans for cost-cutting and improving margins.

Johnston was ostrichlike in not admitting that he needed to find a solution for the company's disappointing earnings, which dropped from $20.5 million, or $2.24 per share in 1984, to $18.5 million, or $1.97 per share in 1985.

As the new chief executive officer of the ad agency, O'-Donnell was determined to figure out why JWT, which was lambasted regularly by the financial community for its low profitability, was not able to make a respectable showing. By going back many years and closely examining the books, O'Donnell found waste and unexplainable extravagance. He questioned the building of a computer compound in Florida for which he could find no rationale. Looking closely at the syndication disaster of 1982, O'Donnell found that the crisis obscured day-to-day problems. When the numbers were restated for the years beginning in 1978, which had phony revenues from the barter syndication unit built in, the new chief executive officer found it peculiar that no one realized how bad 1978, 1979, and 1980 had really been.

O'Donnell also questioned acquisitions that he did not think made good business sense. In 1985 the company acquired or took minority holding companies that cost $7 million, mostly outside the United States. But beyond the range of the worldwide advertising agency, JWT Group made several sizeable acquisitions in 1986. The holding company acquired a market research firm called Winona Inc. and all of the assets of public relations firm Carl Byoir Inc. (an unprofitable firm owned by FCB), together costing $21 million. And in an acquisition many shareholders questioned, JWT bought Grey and Company Public Communications International and merged it into Hill and Knowlton in a deal that exchanged Grey stock for 577,000 shares of JWT common stock, with an additional 94,000 shares reserved for stock options.

The bright but unseasoned O'Donnell was also made aware of practices in JWT's international operations that he found to be irregular. He was disturbed by the practice of paying employees in the company's office in Belgium partly by expense vouchers to help them avoid local taxes. He also found that part of the sum paid to the owners of an ad agency in Turkey purchased by JWT in 1974 was deposited in a Swiss bank account, allegedly to help the owners to avoid local taxes. In the international ad agency community, JWT had the reputation of being one of the "cleanest" in its operations, but O'Donnell nonetheless said he found practices like these morally objectionable.

The first year of O'Donnell's job as chief executive officer was a difficult one for many of JWT's clients, who adjusted their advertising budgets to the competitive environment. Miller Brewing Co., for whom JWT had blasted the "Miller's Made the American Way" message on television and radio to the tune of $75 million the year before, saw no improvement in the plummeting sales of its premium brand Miller High Life. Seeking relief, Miller introduced a new product, Miller Genuine Draft, and the advertising assignment went not to J. Walter Thompson but to Backer & Spielvogel, the Miller Lite agency. The Milwaukee brewer began to deemphasize advertising High Life, and JWT replaced the flag-waving and expensively produced "American Way" campaign with a product story starring actor and former jock Ed Marinaro that looked like it was distilled directly from Coors commercials with Mark Harmon. Genuine Draft got about 40 percent of the ad budget that previously had gone to Thompson, and the New York office was left with a revenue drop.

JWT also lost major accounts, including Champion Spark Plugs, Ryder Truck Rental, Dole fruit products, and Showtime/

The Movie Channel. There were some new accounts joining on in 1986, including Mattel in Europe, Godfather's Pizza, American Greetings in Chicago, and new brands from established clients Warner-Lambert and Quaker Oats.

O'Donnell and his management colleagues in New York decided in mid-1986 to resign the agency's $10 million USAir account in order to pursue the much bigger Continental Airlines business that was up for review. The shortsighted decision was ironic because the very profitable USAir went on to buy two other carriers, which expanded its scope from an East Coast carrier to a truly national airline. And JWT, which got into the running for Continental on the late side, lost the pitch to N W Ayer. Thompson, and especially the Washington office, which had staffed the USAir account, was left with nothing, and the Washington branch was essentially destroyed. Thompson had no choice but to shutter its Washington operation, in the process giving up several other accounts that needed local service and consolidating the rest with the Atlanta branch. It was a humiliating move that undermined staffers' confidence in the still-evolving management team.

For by this time, Manning had left for his new venture, and O'Donnell installed 59-year-old Bertram Metter as chairman of the U.S. company. Metter, a tall, wiry, gray-haired former creative director, had been commanding the agency's new business efforts because he was known for his quick, insightful way of tackling advertising problems and his skills as a penetrating presenter. The departures over the last year of Rydholm, O'Brien, and Manning had thinned the management ranks of veteran admen accustomed to handling problems and clients in the heretofore sacred JWT style.

But the most crushing blow came in October when Kraft, a JWT client since 1922, pulled about $75 million in billings from JWT's Chicago office, leaving only about one fourth of the business that had been built up over the years. Part of the reason was that the general manager who succeeded O'Donnell in Chicago, Don Sullivan, was a deadly choice for the job. JWT had created some terrific advertising for Kraft, and some boring and dated advertising, and the client-agency relationship had been strained during the past few years. O'Donnell, when he was in charge, had taken steps to remedy the situation by installing a new client service team. Ralph Rydholm had tried to stimulate creative solutions to the advertising problems, and prize-winning campaigns—including the commercial set in a diner where all of the customers go for "the soup" instead of chancing a sandwich without Miracle Whip—resulted.

But Sullivan, who came to JWT from Ketchum Communications, San Francisco, did not fit the Thompson mold. A slight, plain, and undistinguished-looking man, Sullivan was said to be abrasive and adversarial with clients rather than acting as a friendly business partner in the O'Donnell style. While the O'Donnell years were known for lavish holiday parties, a shorter work week in the summer, and even Halloween afternoon off for all staffers, Sullivan quickly became known as a stern teetotaler with a strictly business personality.

The chemistry didn't work with the staff, and clients were far from charmed. The Kraft move brought swift staff cuts, and a shiver of fear ran through the Chicago office. Many feared there would be more trouble to come.

As it became clear to O'Donnell that the agency was going to have a dismal year, staff cuts were instituted across the board. JWT paid a total of $5.2 million in severance payments in 1986, which helped to negatively affect the bottom line.

Advertising industry analysts speculated that JWT would have profits of only $10.5 million in 1986, down from $18.5 million the previous year. And in reaction the company's share price slid from the $30 range to the mid-$20s.

If Don Johnston wasn't paying much attention, a financial man from across the Atlantic was watching the situation closely.

It was the opportunistic Martin Sorrell, newly separated from the Saatchis and quickly building his wire-basket shell company through acquisition to a marketing-services holding company named WPP Group.

Sorrell had been swiftly acquiring small, privately held graphics firms, marketing incentives specialists, sales promotion companies, and audiovisual and design outfits in the United Kingdom through early 1986, averaging more than one deal per month. Sorrell showed his determination and ruthlessness in April when he launched a hostile takeover for a publicly held London company, Promotions House. He won control despite the managing director's public threats of a staff walkout.

In the fall of 1986, as he was negotiating a deal with New York's Pace Communications, a consulting firm specializing in the marketing of commercial and residential properties, Sorrell traveled to New York and met with Alan Gottesman, a fast-talking analyst with L. F. Rothschild, Unterberg, Towbin. Gottesman, known to be well acquainted with many of the industry's top executives, agreed to arrange a rendezvous for the British executive with Burt Manning, who had been at his new shop for only a matter of weeks. The very charming Sorrell titillated the egotistically vulnerable Manning with the suggestion that perhaps in the near future and under certain conditions he could return to JWT in victory as its chairman. Manning says he didn't take the possibility too seriously, but Sorrell wasn't speaking lightly.

He had already approached two investment banking firms working with JWT about the idea of a merger.

Johnston was aware of the advances by Sorrell, and he also informed his right-hand man O'Donnell that the company was in play. But Johnston did not respond to Sorrell's advances and instead began, albeit halfheartedly, his secret defense to maintain control of JWT.

At a JWT Group board meeting late in 1986, Johnston convinced his acquiescent board members to pass a buy-back plan for 500,000 shares that was intended to boost the price of the company's stock, and JWT retained takeover defense lawyers Sullivan & Cromwell as a preliminary precautionary measure.

But Johnston clung to the long-held belief that "it could not happen here." A hostile takeover of an advertising agency was always held to be an impossible concept. The conventional thinking was that because the agency had only its people and client loyalty as assets, those would disappear in the face of a takeover threat and the target would be rendered worthless. Johnston arrogantly believed that he had the total support of his company, his board, and his clients, and that without implementing anti-takeover measures in the company's charter or looking for ways to recapitalize, he could still fend off what he considered to be the remote possibility of a takeover threat.

It soon became clear to O'Donnell that JWT's financial performance would be even worse than the dismal predictions of analysts. The actual results for 1986 showed an 11 percent increase in revenue to $649 million but an astonishing 69 percent drop in net income to $5.9 million, or 60 cents per share.

O'Donnell had discovered still more areas of corporate waste that he felt should be controlled, especially in the JWT Group structure. He says he was outraged by the people he found there "saying 'way-to-go' to Johnston, who haven't produced an ad, haven't made any client contact" and were collecting salaries between $200,000 and $300,000 a year. He was starting to believe that the public ownership of the company and its resultant $28 million pre-tax in dividends paid to shareholders was counterproductive for the company.

O'Donnell got together with an old classmate, John Cirigliano, the head of an investment company in New York called Claremont Group. The two concurred with the belief that was now becoming commonplace on Wall Street: if JWT were properly run, it could make many times the profit it had been producing.

On February 3, O'Donnell would take his seat on the JWT Group board of directors for the first time, and as the date approached, the newly installed chairman realized he had to act.

"I was unwilling to sit on the JWT Group board," O'Donnell says. "I was not willing to accept moral and legal responsibility for the decisions they made about the company. They were not a group of people I desired to serve with."

On Tuesday, January 20, O'Donnell asked for a meeting with Johnston, in which he presented to his boss a three-page letter he had received from Cirigliano at Clarement Group.

According to O'Donnell, the letter asked him to take to the board of directors the suggestion that JWT hire the Claremont Group to "come in as consultants and take a look at whether or not [JWT] should be public or private and whether or not [JWT] can do something about it. A report was then going to be made to the board. It was my legal obligation to pass it to Don," O'Donnell says.

At the same time, O'Donnell raised the issue of the company's lack of proper controls under Johnston. He had already discussed his stance on these matters with several key executives in the worldwide ad agency, including Jack Peters, president and chief operating officer; Bert Metter, chairman of the U.S. company; Victor Gutierrez, executive vice-president and financial director, and Lee Preschel, the important president of the Latin American and Central Pacific regions.

And then he went for broke. The 43-year-old O'Donnell, who had been chief executive for less than a year and chairman for twenty days, told a stunned Johnston that "things had to change or I couldn't be a part of them. And amongst [sic] those things that should be considered was Don dropping his line responsibility.

"It was not a demand," the burly O'Donnell says, "but it was a strong suggestion."

"You could have a contract for five or six years," O'Donnell says he told his boss. "You and Ed Ney [chairman of Young & Rubicam] are men of great stature in the business. Coming out of J. Walter Thompson Co. you could take positions that need to be taken in the industry, relative to independence, relative to trust-based relationships between client and agency.

"But in terms of the current line responsibilities in the company that exist, I can't be a part of it."

O'Donnell's hope, of course, was that Johnston would passively step aside into an elder statesman role and let his successor do what he thought was going to help the company return to profitability and a future of independence. But from Johnston's cold reaction, O'Donnell knew that instead, he was going to be fired.

On Thursday, Johnston's secretary asked O'Donnell if he would be available the next day to meet again with Johnston and some of the outside directors. That night, O'Donnell wrote a letter of his own and made sure that it would make its way into the Friday meeting. The letter, which was signed by the Thompson executives who supported him, outlined ten "charges" against Johnston, some of which involved the financial irregularities in foreign operations that O'Donnell had become aware of during the past year. Each charge, according to people who have seen the letter, began with the phrase: "Would you trust a man who . . ."

By convening his supporters on the board, Johnston was both meeting his fiduciary responsibility to hear the proposal from Claremont and mustering support from the only available source. Johnston felt strongly that outside directors, who had backed him through every crisis in his troubled reign, would be there for him again.

The meeting took place on Friday, January 23, with

O'Donnell facing the aging supporters of his mentor-turned-rival. O'Donnell, not a strong public speaker even under the friendliest conditions, was nervous before this hostile group. He put forth the letter he had shown to Johnston and then took his position further.

If taking the agency private was to be the course of action, O'Donnell said in his deliberate manner, he would back the plan only if the majority of the ownership of the company were to be in the hands of the employees and not the managers. Another of his conditions for support of such a proposal, he said, would be that no group of individuals could have such a stake in the company that the first basis of making a decision would be self-interest.

O'Donnell made it clear that he believed deals like the one Bob Jacoby had made for Ted Bates were "obscene." "There's a whole slew of 60-year-old managers who are bailing out of the business and taking the money and screwing the people. It's not right," O'Donnell says he told the board.

Following his impassioned but somewhat disconnected presentation, O'Donnell was asked to leave the boardroom. O'Donnell says he still doesn't know if he was fired by Johnston or by the board.

The crisis again called for Hill & Knowlton's special situations unit, this time under the direction of the firm's chairman Bob Dilenschneider.

Over the weekend, Dilenschneider tracked down advertising reporters around the country. "Are you sitting down?" he began. "Do I have a story for you!"

The barrage of publicity surrounding O'Donnell's ouster was carefully crafted by the Hill & Knowlton team, who were accomplished at shaping coverage of corporate troubles. The party line went that O'Donnell had submitted an unsolicited buyout bid from Claremont and that he had asked for Johnston's job. Hill & Knowlton made available certain board members, such as David Yunich, the 69-year-old director since Johnston's tenure began in 1974, who gleefully vilified O'Donnell in the press.

Johnston and his support group attributed O'Donnell's mistakes to his having been "just an office manager" before being appointed to head the worldwide company. Dilenschneider and his team encouraged reporters to believe characterizations of O'Donnell as being impatient, disloyal, greedy, and backstabbing, while O'Donnell himself was barely commenting except to say that the JWT allegations were not true.

Two months before his sixtieth birthday, Johnston reassumed the position of chairman and chief executive officer of J. Walter Thompson Co. His press agents made him available for interviews in the office that O'Donnell had occupied, in which he would not discuss anything about the ouster of his handpicked successor. He put up a falsely cheerful front for all to see, saying he was "back in the business," and although this was a hardship in personal terms because it interfered with his planned retirement, he was delighted to have the chance to "stabilize the company."

His first acts after moving back into the corner office were to fire gradually all of the executives who had backed O'Donnell. Peters, a thirty-year company veteran, was out within days. Although Johnston said at the time that there would be no other dismissals, Gutierrez, Preschel, and Metter were all purged from the company.

With Peters gone, Johnston said that not only would he be chairman of the holding company and chairman of the advertising agency, he would also take the chief operating officer role in Peters's absence.

While morale at the agency plummeted as employees reeled in confusion about the events, the agency's stock price climbed amid takeover talk. Competitors on Madison Avenue, themselves shocked by such a public airing of inner turmoil, drooled over the new business opportunities Johnston was dishing up for them. IBM, Burger King, and Ford Motor Co.—three of Thompson's most important and prestigious accounts—were rumored to be halfway out the door of the commotion-wracked agency.

If Johnston had thought ignoring Sorrell's overtures months before would keep the matter of JWT's vulnerability quiet, his decision to make his battle with O'Donnell public had the opposite effect. The open display of hostilities called attention to all of JWT's weaknesses—its dismal earnings picture, its lack of management depth, and the instability that made it a perfect target for an outside company that wanted to dive into mega-merger frenzy.

CHAPTER 16

"**J**WT Group is not for sale, none of JWT Group's companies are for sale, nor are any parts of JWT Group companies for sale," Don Johnston said to the crowd at the company's May 5, 1987, annual meeting.

In the customary setting of the McGraw-Hill Building's auditorium on Sixth Avenue and Forty-ninth Street, Johnston faced angry shareholders, inquisitive analysts, and a fascinated press corps to explain the tumult that had engulfed the agency that was once as solid as the Rock of Gibraltar, which it had made a symbol for the Prudential Life Insurance Co. in 1896.

Just a year earlier in the same room, Johnston had heralded the ascension of a new management lineup at the holding company's flagship agency, starring the attractive and promising Joe O'Donnell and his teammate Jack Peters. Now they had been expelled in disgrace, having challenged Johnston's ability to lead the company, and the chairman was left alone to defend JWT's poor performance and his own disintegrating reputation.

"For JWT Group Inc.," Johnston said, "the last 12 months have been a period of much public frustration and some significant, less widely publicized accomplishments. The frustrations have all been clearly spelled out in the press; several key management appointments went sour and advertising budgets around the world did not live up to early expectations. By the time we were in a position to make cost cuts commensurate with budget decreases, it was already too late to salvage profit levels."

Johnston attacked the megamerger trend, disparaging the "currently popular activity in which large advertising agencies disappear into each other."

"What all this loses sight of is the essence of an advertising agency, which is a service business, a business that prospers or fails based on how effectively it services its clients. In all the megamerger frenzy and excitement, there is very little that is of benefit to clients. In many cases, exactly the opposite is true, as clients are well aware. In fact, megamergers have raised in many clients' minds profound questions about the loyalty and professional commitment of their agencies. This has induced an unusually high degree of client turnover.

"The Thompson company," Johnston said, "has no intention of participating in this mating of giants. It doesn't need to. Thompson has grown over the course of 122 years, one account at a time, one office at a time, one country at a time. . . . Rather than attempting to grow via megamerger, we intend to maintain Thompson's identity as 'advertising's leading brand' with all that that means in terms of coherent professional philosophy and a distinct corporate culture.

"On a personal note," Johnston said at the conclusion of his chairman's address, "I began this past year with high hopes for the promise of a new management in J. Walter Thompson Company, and I am deeply saddened that this promise was not realized. Yet, over and over again, the support received from our clients and the loyalty and commitment of J. Walter Thompson men and women all over the world have been deeply gratifying. Professional strength and resiliency are built into the fiber of this company; they give me the confidence to look forward to a better 1987."

Ironically, on the day the JWT shareholders were hearing Johnston's apologies for the company's performance, the advertising column in the *New York Times* led with a story about Joe O'Donnell, who had already landed a new job as chief executive officer of the former Ted Bates subsidiary William Esty Co. that now reported directly to Saatchi & Saatchi Communications. O'Donnell had been hired to harness the decline of the ailing agency that had been struck by client defections from the Bates megamerger. And within a month of his arrival, conditions took an extreme turn for the worse. Esty, in a move that O'Donnell said took him entirely by surprise, was fired by its biggest client, Nissan Motor Corp., with a $140 million budget, and the largest single account loss in the history of advertising. The column by Philip H. Dougherty presented O'Donnell's rationale for resigning the $40 million MasterCard International account rather than participate in the review it was sure to lose.

Though O'Donnell now had new management challenges of his own to wrestle with, including cutting the agency's 440-person staff by one third, he had not been mistaken about the profitability picture of his alma mater. At the same time as Johnston was spouting his stoic philosophy, the company was reporting a net loss for the second consecutive quarter. JWT Group lost $1.4 million in the first quarter of 1987, while revenues for the period ended on March 31 increased from $151.2 million to $159.6 million.

That did not stop Johnston, however, from telling the hundreds of people at the annual meeting that the company would have earnings of $2.00 per share, the 1985 level, by the end of the year. When an analyst posed a pointed question, asking the chairman how he expected to accomplish this in light of the just-reported loss, his answer was symbolic of the arrogant and out-of-touch ruler he had become. We don't have to explain our plans to you, is essentially what Johnston said.

An officer of the company, in retrospect, pointed out that Johnston probably knew at that point he wouldn't be around to have to fulfill his promised projections.

The upheaval at JWT told Martin Sorrell that it was time to pursue again, but this time he was to take a stealthy approach. A takeover of a company the size of JWT, which dwarfed his own, would have been part of Sorrell's strategy for growth several years down the road, he explained. But the lack of management strength, exemplified by the number of top executives dismissed, amazed the 42-year-old Englishman. "Well over 100 years of experience has been jettisoned from the company," Sorrell said.

Just weeks after O'Donnell's ouster, Martin Sorrell met with a takeover specialist of the British merchant bank Samuel Montagu & Co., Rupert Faure Walker. Over breakfast in the London banking firm's private dining room, the team planned how the little minnow from London could devour the bloated American fish. They set up a joint company called Tiptree and, largely financed by Samuel Montagu, began assembling a stake in the company at a price averaging $30 per share. The American unit of Sorrell's company, established for the same purpose, was called the Owl Group, a playful poke at the longtime JWT symbol.

One week after Johnston promised a sound and prosperous year for the company, Burger King Corp., a $200 million account in the New York office that accounted for one third of that operation's revenues, announced it needed new advertising and marketing solutions and was putting its business up for review. Though the competition would be a prolonged affair with a decision not expected until the fall, the revelation that Johnston did not have a firm grip on even the biggest of his clients put JWT in an even more precarious situation.

At the same time that Sorrell was building his stake to 478,100 shares, or just under the 5 percent level that requires disclosure to the Securities and Exchange Commission, other parties were accumulating their holdings as well. These turned out to be the brokerage firm Bear Stearns, which said its interest was purely as an investment, and a group headed by former Ted Bates executive John Hoyne and financially backed by Bob Jacoby.

As the trading volume pushed the price higher, speculation surfaced on Wall Street about a takeover attempt. Johnston issued statements to his company saying that he knew nothing about such an attempt, which technically could have been true because no group had reached the 5 percent mark. And as rumors increased in New York, JWT spokesman Don Deaton, the same Hill & Knowlton executive who had publicly defended the company against the taint of Marie Luisi and had helped to spread the word about O'Donnell's supposed attempted coup, said, "It's all news to us."

And as speculation increased, Johnston sent a memorandum to the company pledging that he was certain the best course for JWT was to "remain independent."

But on June 8, unbeknownst to the company at large or to shareholders, the board of directors had swiftly implemented "golden parachute" provisions for twenty-six officers and key employees of the company, calling for them to receive 2.9 times their annual compensation in cash if they were to leave the company for any reason other than death, retirement, cause, or disability within two years of a "change in control" at JWT. Johnston, it was agreed, would receive only twice his annual compensation of $700,000. The golden parachutes were approved both to protect current executives and to make the company more expensive for a prospective suitor.

On Wednesday, June 10, Johnston and the board of directors received a letter from Martin Sorrell, whose own company had 1986 revenues of $38 million and net income of $1.6 million, offering to buy all of the outstanding stock of JWT (which had 1986 revenues of $649 million) for $45 per share, or $460 million, in cash.

The move hearkened back to the days when Charles Saatchi, then the owner of a tiny agency with only one office in London, would impertinently send off letters to his competitors offering to buy them. But Don Johnston was not in a position to indignantly turn Martin Sorrell down flat. JWT stock had climbed, because of speculation about a possible takeover, to about $40 per share, and JWT was compelled to consider the offer.

Johnston heard the news Wednesday morning in London where he was on company business, just as Martin Sorrell was boarding the British Airways Concorde to meet the business day in New York and start negotiations there. JWT retained Morgan Stanley & Co. at a fee of $1 million to be its financial advisor and consider the offer.

"We have the greatest admiration for the history, tradition and professional strengths of JWT, and particularly respect its creative talent and reputation for effective advertising and not least your personal contribution," Sorrell wrote to Johnston. But the cunning businessman then threw in the angle that was sure to inflame the JWT chief. "For these reasons we have arranged for Jack Peters, who has experience of over 30 years with JWT, to come back to JWT in a senior management capacity following the consummation of our proposed merger."

Sorrell had hooked up with Peters just after he was purged from Thompson and used his knowledge of the company as a tool in putting together his takeover strategy. Peters, who still was being paid his $450,000 annual salary by JWT until the day of Sorrell's letter, when he notified JWT to cease payments, was to receive $1,233 per day from Sorrell's company until the acquisition negotiations were completed. He was contractually promised the job of president and chief operating officer at a minimum salary of $500,000 a year if the deal went through, plus a $1.35 million bonus if he stayed on through 1990. Even if Sorrell was not successful in his bid for JWT, Peters would collect $1.3 million over three years.

Thus the crafty Sorrell tried to make his bid more palatable to JWT clients who might balk at the idea of a hostile takeover, by saying that Peters's involvement made the deal a management buyout. It was evident from the outset, however, that if Peters came back, Johnston would be paid to depart. "It is unlikely that Peters and Johnston would ride in the same elevator," said an industry analyst at the time.

From his base of operations in New York, the elegantly dated Mayfair Regent hotel just around corner from the posh boutiques of Madison Avenue, Sorrell huddled with his financial advisors, fielded phone calls, and waited for Johnston's response. He made it clear, in free-ranging interviews taken in the hotel's lounge with a constantly ringing telephone and a stack of unanswered messages at his side, that he was quite willing to negotiate in a friendly manner with JWT, but if the company did not respond, he would launch a $45-per-share tender offer within days.

On Friday morning, June 12, Sorrell did indeed take his bid for JWT Group directly to shareholders, while the company's financial advisors evaluated the bid. WPP Group, through its British bankers and Credit Suisse and First Boston, had obtained commitments to raise $530 million in financing for the deal. Just as in the acquisitions he had engineered for Saatchi & Saatchi in its quick rise to dominance in the worldwide advertising industry, Sorrell's plan was to finance the deal, not through assuming a massive debt that would have put pressure on the newly acquired company to generate a quick cash flow to meet payments, but through the uniquely British technique of the rights issue. WPP shareholders would have the right to purchase more shares at a reduced rate, thus generating cash for the company.

JWT Group rejected the $45-per-share offer, deeming it inadequate and urging shareholders not to tender their stock.

And on June 15, the highly charged negotiations began to escalate as Sorrell presented the possibility of a $50.50-per-share offer and JWT began looking for a white knight, a friendly company that would buy JWT with management support.

The next two weeks were filled with suits and countersuits by both parties, one in particular from JWT focusing on the involvement of Peters and his alleged disclosure of confidential information to WPP.

Johnston finally gave up using the word "independence" in his regular and uninformative updates to the company, telling them not to believe stories in the press and that he was determined to maintain the company's "integrity."

"We're single-minded. We're committed. We're determined. And we've got a number of balls in the air," Johnston wrote to his employees.

Several of JWT's important clients, meanwhile, made public and inflamatory statements about their feelings regarding the takeover attempt, both in a show of support for Johnston and in revulsion for the trend that was taking them out of the driver's seat in agency-client relationships. Goodyear Tire & Rubber Co. was one of the first to react. Itself the victim of a bitter takeover battle with Sir James Goldsmith, which pulled Goodyear apart despite its eventual victory, the Akron, Ohio, company's vice-president of advertising James DeVoe went on the record the day after Sorrell's initial letter saying that if Sorrell were successful, the account would be reviewed.

Another client with close ties to Johnston, Eastman-Kodak Co., said it would view any change in Thompson's management and ownership as "negative and disruptive." And Ford Motor Co., the agency's biggest client, with $300 million in billings around the world, put out a statement that said Ford "is concerned that any change in [JWT's] corporate structure or management team could have a detrimental effect on the agency's relationship with Ford division.

"If there were a change in JWT ownership or senior management, it would cause an agency review by Ford division."

While investment bank Morgan Stanley tried to drum up some interest from other outside investors, Johnston's priority was just what had gotten Joe O'Donnell booted out of the company in disgrace months before. Johnston wanted to return to private ownership, a course that would probably necessitate the sell-off of some of the smaller subsidiaries to their managements. But in the face of a bid that had already lined up its financing commitments, JWT management could find no one to lend them the money.

"JWT does not have the credit-worthiness to do it," said Charles Crane, an analyst with Prudential Bache Securities. "The more [subsidiaries] they sell, the more feasible it would become. If they sold everything but J. Walter Thompson Co., they would need $350 million. Which would mean they'd have to have $60 million in cash flow, which is more than what they make."

As the company's share price climbed higher through June on expectations that Sorrell would raise his bid, the possibility of a Johnston-led management team being able to convince a banker to lend him the money given his own dreadful financial management record disappeared into thin air.

Despite much speculation about white knights, ranging from a Rockefeller Group venture-capital fund and to some interest from the founder of MTV: Music Television, Robert Pittman, backed by his new employer MCA Inc., when the JWT Group board convened in the early evening of June 25, there were only two bids on the table.

JWT stock was trading at around $52 per share. The investment group represented by Lazard Frères included the cash-heavy John Hoyne and Bruce McLaren, both formerly of Ted Bates, who were eager to install themselves as the new top management team at JWT. They claimed that their former boss and current plotting partner Bob Jacoby was not involved in the deal except as an investor. But many, including the JWT board members, knew Jacoby's reputation well enough to believe his denials of personal involvement were only due to the fact that he was still contractually bound to Saatchi & Saatchi, still collecting his salary and awaiting word on the arbitration of his breached contract. Jacoby was to put up $10 million in cash. Hoyne and his partners were offering $55 per share, in cash, for JWT.

The board members, led by a beaten Don Johnston, gathered over a dinner of sandwiches and beer and deliberated for seven hours. As the meeting drew to a close, Hayne believed he had succeeded in beating Sorrell for control of the $3 billion agency.

But Johnston, aware of how Jacoby and the Bates-Saatchi deal had so infuriated clients, including the important account Warner-Lambert, resisted closing the deal with the former Bates executives. Sorrell contends that his $55.50 bid went into the room at the 6 P.M. deadline. "We knew there would be a $55 bid," he says, "and that others would tend to think in round numbers." Sorrell says he was not prepared to go as high as $60, and believed a slight premium over Hoyne's bid would win because of the "genuine horror" the board felt at the prospect of an affiliation with Jacoby. The JWT board agreed—on the condition that Peters would not be permitted to run the company. According to Sorrell, the agreement was reached by 11 P.M. and the drained legal and financial advisors met at the law offices of Sullivan & Cromwell to draw up the final papers.

J. Walter Thompson, the 123-year-old bastion of American advertising, had given up its independence to a minute British conqueror who manufactured wire shopping baskets, for $566 million.

Though Johnston escaped the initial humiliation of his rival Jack Peters returning to Thompson, the chairman had no inkling that Sorrell had another surprise waiting in the wings.

Nor were the partners or the clients of the man who would be the third chairman of J. Walter Thompson Co. in a one-year period aware that he would be leaving their enterprise after less than a year to return to the agency that had built his career. For Burt Manning had assured his clients and his partners at Jordan, Manning, Case, Taylor & McGarth, which had grown with new assignments from Quaker Oats Co. and other clients thanks to Manning's contacts, that he would be remaining with them no matter what the situation at JWT.

Two weeks later, on the day WPP Group closed its $55.50-per-share tender offer and took control, Sorrell announced the new management structure. JWT Group was eliminated—and with it Johnston's role as chairman and chief executive officer. The chief executives of each of the units—Lord Geller Federico Einstein, Hill & Knowlton, MRB Research, and J. Walter Thompson Co.—would report to Sorrell. And the new chairman and chief executive officer of J. Walter Thompson Co. was to be Burt Manning, who was already back in the Park Avenue Atrium offices the day his move appeared as a leak in the *New York Times*.

There was no role for Johnston in the British-owned corporation, a fact that had been apparent since the deal was signed, but he stayed on, a pariah, under financial obligation to Sorrell to give the appearance of stability for the sake of the clients and the WPP investment. Johnston moved out of the corner office he had appropriated from O'Donnell into a smaller room down the hall. He received no mail, few phone calls, and fewer visitors. The 60-year-old adman still believed that the new rulers would look to him for support and counsel, but instead he was pointedly ignored until, with no fanfare and not even an internal announcement, he slipped away on October 31, 1987.

Manning, with no support from a chief operating officer, few close management allies aside from those in the U.S. company, and no mentor to lead the way, was to oversee an agency with 10,000 employees and offices in forty countries.

And soon the bloodletting began. Sorrell and Manning toured the U.S. to Rochester and Detroit and Akron, the headquarters cities of their concerned clients, assuring them that all would be well. Manning, they promised, would continue the traditions of JWT, with no cutbacks in service or quality despite the legions of Sorrell's financial men who were infiltrating the agencies' offices. But who will run the company, clients wanted to know. JWT was now on the defensive, having to protect itself against the clients' mistrust and the onslaught of its voracious competitors, themselves trying to grow in a difficult advertising environment.

Swiftly and mercilessly, and before the acquisition had been completed, Ford Motor Co., one of the most important clients of JWT in Europe, pulled $110 million in international advertising billings from Thompson, splitting the business between Ogilvy & Mather and Young & Rubicam. JWT, which created the trademark "Have you driven a Ford lately?" campaign, lost the automaker's accounts in nine European countries and in Canada, fueling deep concern on the part of JWT management about the future of the account in the U.S. Ford contended publicly that the move was not related to the acquisition.

The Burger King competition made clear a new condition of the post-megamerger advertising world. Although the account was to have billings of $200 million, there were few large agencies that were available to handle it, because of competitive accounts within their own systems. The final shootout involved D'Arcy Masius Benton & Bowles and N W Ayer, with JWT working at a clear disadvantage. The Miami-based subsidiary of Pillsbury had been unhappy with JWT since the ill-fated "Herb the Nerd" campaign, which had been a critical and business bomb. When Burger King introduced the nebbish who had never had a Whopper in the fall of 1985, Burt Manning, then chairman and chief creative officer of JWT, ballyhooed the idea in his many public speaking engagements as one of the best efforts in the fast-food industry. JWT had trouble recouping its status as a strong creative shop in the minds of the Burger King clients, because it was unable to develop an enduring campaign as a followup, and went from one weak strategy to another over the next year and a half.

By the time the shootout came, with Manning newly installed in the company's top post, JWT had been trimmed and purged to the extent that its resources were not sufficiently deep to fight a strong fight. The pitch team recruited contributions from the agency's other offices, all of which were still shellshocked from the events of the summer. On the eve of the decision, Manning sent a message to the staff thanking them for their efforts and saying that JWT "deserved to win."

But JWT lost the account to N W Ayer, a privately held independent shop that had been growing steadily over the past year despite the disappointing loss of its U.S. Army recruitment account. With one third of the revenues gone from the New York office effective with the Burger King departure, JWT, now more cost-conscious than ever, instantly fired about one hundred people.

The next blow came quickly when Goodyear announced that it was dropping JWT on the biggest part of its business, the national advertising business for tires, a $25 million budget handled out of New York. JWT had created strong campaigns for Goodyear, especially the sensitive "Goodyear take me home" spots that had been winning critical acclaim. Manning and Sorrell could have saved face and resigned the account early on, rather than letting the agency be strung along after the client's public statements about British ownership. And Goodyear made the firing worse by blurring the issue of foreign control by retaining JWT's Detroit office for special ads for racing tires and the Brouillard Communications subsidiary for corporate advertising.

After a quick competition, Young & Rubicam, the biggest privately held independent agency, won the account.

The Chicago office of JWT, the agency's biggest in the early 1980s, also experienced the painful process of a rapidly shrinking billings base in the first months of a new management team's reign. The unpopular Don Sullivan was taken out of his general manager post and given an inside job in strategic planning to fulfill his contract, while one of the agency's former co–creative directors, veteran Thompsonite Alan Webb, was put in the top Chicago spot. Within a one month period in the fall following the acquisition, JWT/Chicago gave up $13 million in billings from S. C. Johnson & Son's hair-care products (Agree: "Turn up the volume in your hair") and another $10 million–plus from Beatrice's Hunt/Wesson division's specialty foods, such as LaChoy, Rosarita, and Fisher Nut brands.

Chicago, too, had to face the painful reality of competing for an important account it had little chance of retaining. JWT was the agency to develop all of the introductory strategies and advertising for Sears, Roebuck & Co.'s Discover Card, part of the giant retailer's push into financial services under its Dean Witter unit. JWT's advertising was lackluster, but Sears is a notoriously difficult client, and the fault may not have been entirely with the agency. Nevertheless, in the midst of Thompson's turmoil, Dean Witter management said it wanted new thinking as the card rolled from its introductory phase to its adolescence. JWT's "Dawn of Discover" ads had been effective in putting cards into customers' wallets, but not in getting them to the cash register. The $40 million account went up for review against the two strong creative shops in Chicago: DDB Needham and Leo Burnett Co. With morale at an all-time low at JWT due to several waves of staff cuts during the summer and little hope of holding on to Discover, it would have been expected that Manning, in his role as chairman of the company, would come to Chicago to lend a hand or to appear at the pitch. The

JWT chairman, however, was jetting around the world putting out local fires, getting to know international clients for the first time, and had no time for Chicago.

At DDB Needham, on the other hand, Keith Reinhard, whose worldwide problems in merging two agencies matched those of Manning, did take the time to put his hand into the agency's pitch and to appear at the final meeting. DDB Needham won the Discover Card account.

Alan Webb's internal announcement about the loss of business, on the heels of the other account moves weeks earlier, did little to minimize its seriousness and indicated that another wave of staff cuts and cost-cutting would undoubtedly follow.

And the Pepsi-Cola Co., which five years ago was becoming an important client of JWT, also issued a stinging blow in November when it switched a major piece of its international business from Thompson to its favorite agency BBDO. BBDO, Pepsi figured, was producing all of the great "Taste of a new generation" commercials with hot stars ranging from Michael J. Fox to Michael Jackson, which were popular with Pepsi bottlers all over the world. BBDO was given "headquarters" responsibility for developing global ad campaigns that local bottlers everywhere, from Latin America to the Far East, could use if they chose. This contact with the local markets also gives BBDO a chance to make further headway against Thompson in gaining the accounts of the bottlers in distant markets.

JWT had worked closely with Pepsi in the early 1980s, developing a new kind of soft drink that the dynamic president of Pepsi U.S.A., Roger Enrico, believed could capture 10 percent of the $35 billion soda market. Slice, Thompson named it, a juice-added refreshing drink that would capitalize on the health-consciousness of young Americans. Thompson introduced Slice as a test-market product with the line "We've got the juice," and Pepsi quickly took the product into national distribution with a wide range of flavors. The product caught on to the point that it inspired many copycats, and Slice was not able to maintain its original share of the market.

In November 1987, Pepsi told JWT it would have to fight for the $25 million Slice budget against the toughest of rivals: BBDO. And again the weakened JWT lost. By the end of 1987, J. Walter Thompson Co. had lost close to $500 million in billings around the world. Its Chicago operation dropped from a strong number two to number four in the market, while New York billings shrank to about $350 million, no longer a significant factor in the world's biggest advertising city. Sorrell counters these losses with evidence that the agency has picked up about $300 million in additional billings from clients and from new business, contending that the net loss of $150 million is not significant compared to the total revenues of the group he purchased.

By the first weeks of 1988, Manning and Sorrell purged five other top JWT executives who had been loyal to Johnston, and whose jobs no longer figured in their plans: John Cronin, vice chairman, Harry Clark, executive vice president, Terence Martin, chief financial officer, Steven Salorio, general counsel, and Ron Kovas, a former director of JWT Group—all of whom were believed to be covered by golden parachutes.

What was the signal that some of the biggest advertisers in America were sending Thompson? That what they value in an agency is integrity, stability, creativity, and concentration on their business.

A management-poor agency, torn by politics and the struggle for profits, is no match for those who keep their eye steadily on the client's ball.

While the turmoil at J. Walter Thompson Co. was the most public manifestation of the trouble in the WPP world, a more private battle was fermenting at Sorrell's Lord Geller Federico Einstein subsidiary.

The "premium brand" agency, as former JWT Group chairman Johnston called it, Lord Geller had become renowned for its outstanding advertising for IBM's personal computers. The long-lived campaign used the character of Charlie Chaplain's Little Tramp to personalize the concept of computers to prospective customers.

Lord Geller was launched in 1967 by Richard Lord, a well-respected writer who had worked at Young & Rubicam, Benton & Bowles, and Warwick Advertising. His partners included an outstanding art director, Gene Federico, who would be elected to the Art Directors Hall of Fame.

Reaching $5 million in billings by 1974 with accounts like Hennessey cognac, Elizabeth Arden, and Tiffany, the Lord Geller partners realized they needed an alliance with a bigger agency to be able to attract major clients. Don Johnston, impressed by Lord's talents and his personal style—a combination of street smarts and urbanity—agreed to buy Lord Geller Federico Einstein and make it an autonomous subsidiary of JWT Group.

Lord Geller grew to be a $220 million agency, with IBM's $100-million budget becoming its most important client. As the agency became bigger and more successful, the partners chafed under JWT ownership, as their prospects for new accounts were limited by potential conflicts with JWT.

The prestige automaker Jaguar, for example, wanted Lord Geller to handle its account in America, but had to be turned away because of sister agency JWT's relationship with Ford Motor Co. Fuji Photo Film U.S.A. became a client after much wrangling over the position of Kodak at JWT, but Lord Geller handled only videotape products and was barred from pitching film brands.

Lord and his partners wanted to buy back the agency from Johnston. They developed business plans that brought up the possibility of the agency's existing on its own, possibly without the IBM account, and discussed the contingencies with Johnston. Once Sorrell took over, they were even more determined to regain ownership of their agency.

Sorrell saw Lord Geller as one of the most treasured prizes in the JWT Group acquisition because it earned the highest profit margins of any division as well as being prestigious because of its creative reputation.

The Lord Geller executive committee met repeatedly following the June 1987 takeover to discuss the future relationship of the agency and its parent, WPP Group. The Lord Geller partners were clearly displeased with issues involving employment contracts, phantom stock plan, profit sharing, employee bonuses, and a new incentive program. They outlined several possible future scenarios, including trying to split ownership with Sorrell, with WPP as the minority partner. On several occasions the executive committee members asked Sorrell to sell Lord Geller to them. "My response consistently was Lord Geller is not for sale," Sorrell says.

Nevertheless, beginning in the fall of 1987, Lord and his partners had several meetings in the Sky Club of the Pan Am Building with officials of the biggest American ad agency, Young & Rubicam, including its chairman Alex Kroll. The discussions involved Young & Rubicam's providing financial help for the leaders of Lord Geller to buy themselves back from WPP Group. The investment firm of Dean Witter, a Lord Geller client, also was assisting with the preparation of a presentation to Sorrell on the subject of a management buyout.

Sorrell continued to refuse to discuss the sale of the agency.

At the same time, the principals of Lord Geller were negotiating employment contracts with WPP, in which the question of the agency's autonomy became a key issue. Lord says Sorrell withheld 1987 employee bonuses to coerce the principals to sign.

Sorrell, meanwhile, had widely spoken of his idea to establish a European network of ad agencies that would bear the Lord

Geller name, and he had done so despite Lord's rejection of the plan. Sorrell's intention was to employ European JWT execs under the LGFE banner, to work on the Alpha Romeo account. Additionally, Sorrell had ordered Lord to withdraw from the competition for the $100-million account to handle advertising for the upcoming Saturn division of General Motors, which would be considered to be a conflict by JWT client Ford Motor Co. Lord told the *Wall Street Journal* of his displeasure with these situations and was censured by an angry Sorrell.

On March 11, 1988, the question of selling Lord Geller to its managing partners was again brought to Sorrell, this time by representatives of First Boston, the investment banking firm that had advised him during the takeover of JWT Group, and at the urging of Lord's lawyers. Sorrell's refusal to discuss the plan this final time proved to Lord and his partners they had to act.

Sorrell flew to New York from London on the morning of March 18, sensing trouble because Lord had not been returning his telephone calls. "I told him that I was here to meet with him and the other members of the Executive Committee at any time convenient to them," Sorrell said in a court affidavit. "I explained that I had some proposals that might interest them. Mr. Lord replied, 'Maybe the house has burned down.' I pleaded with him to set up a meeting with the Executive Committee. I said that even if they did not want to speak with me, I had things I wanted to say to them. I told him that I had put together a presentation that I believed would be a fair and reasonable solution.

"The next and last thing I heard from the management I had entrusted to run Lord Geller was an envelope containing the simultaneous resignations of all six, effective immediately."

Richard J. Lord, Arthur W. Einstein, Kevin B. O'Neill, Edward D. Yaconetti, Conrad Freeman, and Lewis E. Eichenholtz, the key executives at Lord Geller, walked out on Sorrell that Friday morning, leaving behind a memo for their staff. Within hours they announced the formation of a new advertising agency, called Lord, Einstein, O'Neill & Partners, adding that Young & Rubicam was to be a minority partner in the firm.

The 300 or so staffers at Lord Geller were in shock, as were the agency's clients.

Over the weekend Sorrell had meetings with executives who remained, trying to set up an organizational structure. Monday morning Gene Federico and Norman Geller, older men who were brought back from their relatively inactive roles, announced a new management committee of account and creative-group department heads, who would "ensure the continuity of our operations." That evening most of the people on the management committee told Sorrell they were resigning, too.

Several of the agency's clients, including *The New Yorker* magazine and WNBC-TV, announced their intention to move to the newly formed shop. Sorrell threw himself into a frenzy of activity, phoning clients at their homes and in their vacation spots, begging them to remain with what was left of his possession.

As many as fifty employees of LGFE followed Lord to his new agency in the first week. Fuji gave Lord Geller notice that it was terminating its agency relationship agreement. The vice president of advertising and promotion for Sony Corp. of America wrote to acting managing director William Wardell, expressing the company's concern about the agency's ability to continue to provide a high level of creativity and service. Wardell announced the resignation of the Sony account over the issue of agency compensation.

And LGFE's biggest client, IBM, demanded in a sternly worded letter that Martin Sorrell provide, within forty-eight hours of the receipt of its March 23 message, a detailed "organization chart with the names and titles of the people you assign to the IBM team as well as the specific skills and relevant experience they bring to the significant projects we are facing in the immediate future."

Martin Sorrell, under the aegis of his U.S. subsidiary Owl Group, filed suit in New York State Supreme Court against the six defecting executives and Young & Rubicam, claiming they conspired to damage the business of LGFE. He asked that they be stopped from taking clients and personnel from the agency he owned and that they be prohibited from using the name "Lord" in their new agency's name.

In the initial days of the legal battle Sorrell released to the press memos he said Lord's people had left behind that allegedly proved his conspiracy charges and cast the well-thought-of Dick Lord and his partners in the most negative light. True, the executives at LGFE had been planning for a way out. Lord, too tough and too smart to be "treated like a piece of furniture" by Sorrell, however, was determined to do business his own way.

Few who know Lord and Alex Kroll at Y&R believe the executives would have acted carelessly or without sound advice from legal counsel. Lord and his partners had not signed employment contracts with Sorrell. Their noncompete agreements dated back to those signed with JWT in 1974, for a period of five years.

The public battle drew daily attention to the troubles of the advertising world, and to the turmoil caused by takeovers.

Just as in the months previous, when JWT was beset by unrest, competitors circled over the prime client pickings and gossip swirled from London to Manhattan.

And yet another great agency was plunged into an unalterable tailspin.

CHAPTER 17

"Some people believe that the only thing Omnicom has produced is Omniphobia," Keith Reinhard says.

Reinhard's dream of melding the two cultures of Doyle Dane Bernbach and Needham Harper Worldwide, he admits now, was a naive one. "As I explored options for our company I sold myself on the idea," Reinhard says. "Over and over I looked at reels from the two agencies, studied quotes from Bernbach and Harper."

The ultimate idealist, who therefore believes others share his visions, Reinhard was sure that the combination would create a positive synergy.

"Somebody said the only place they actually saw synergy work was in a crossword puzzle," Reinhard said, disillusioned, a year later.

The forced combination failed to create a stronger agency, and, Reinhard learned, "to a large number of people, instead of getting the best of both worlds, you get nothing."

"Change creates trauma," Reinhard now says, and nowhere in the megamerger scene was there more trauma than at DDB Needham.

Reinhard calls himself "inclusionist"—everybody has something to bring to the party, he believes. "But New York arrogance doesn't even acknowledge anything going on anywhere else, and Chicago had a surprising and unexplainable complex," he says in explaining DDB problems.

In September 1986, a scaled-down Needham Harper Worldwide New York staff moved into already cramped Doyle Dane Bernbach offices on Madison Avenue between Forty-ninth and Fiftieth streets, and culture clash began in earnest. There were too many top executives—seven executive vice-president–creative directors alone reported to one executive creative director. The Needham invader Tony Vanderwarker had built his career in the Chicago office and was a favorite of Reinhard's. Keith had brought Vanderwarker to Needham, New York, as the top creative man when he was striving desperately to build the office through new business. Vanderwarker's background was as a producer—the person who works with outside directors on the business end and the nitty-gritty of commercial production. In the DDB culture, producers did not have the respect that the cult of the writer or art director had. Some of the top names at DDB—Helmut Krone and Robert Gage—who were now peers of Vanderwarker in the corporate structure, never used producers in their own work. After three months, during which he said he was receiving threats of bodily harm, Vanderwarker started talking to his friends in Chicago who were negotiating to buy the Backer & Spielvogel branch there from Saatchi & Saatchi. DDB Needham lost two of its valued executives, Vanderwarker and Ron Bess, who headed the Anheuser-Busch account, to that independent venture.

Reinhard tried to demonstrate the "best of both worlds" concept by getting several of the offices involved to solve a creative problem for one of DDB's most important accounts, Audi of America. The assignment for a new campaign—to counter Audi's terrible image problem associated with its accidental acceleration recalls—went out to Chicago, Los Angeles, Detroit, and New York. Reinhard himself played the role of creative director, pulling in the best of the ideas to create the campaign. Creative people, in general, detest such a "gangbang." Writers and art directors who have worked on a particular account the longest believe they know the most about how to solve the problem and are offended that others have the chance to put their stamp on the advertising. Creatives from outside the account see gangbangs as a chance to get their ideas noticed, but they must add this assignment to all of the others that their regular accounts demand and usually end up putting in all-nighters to make the presentation deadline. No creative person is happy when individual ideas are plucked from different campaigns to form one. Then no one can claim authorship and no one feels impelled to make the final product conform to his or her strong original vision.

"You're ready for an Audi" was the campaign that won the competition, and it came from the Chicago office. The marketing executives at Audi headquarters in Detroit were pleased with the result, and a shaky account would not be looking to other agencies. Chicago won creative responsibility for the Audi account from that time on, a great accomplishment for them that was viewed as an affront in New York. Reinhard held up this instance of pooling creative resources to skeptical clients as an example of the benefit of the merger, but internally it served to exacerbate the problem of trying to unite the agencies.

The international offices of Doyle Dane Bernbach and Needham Harper Worldwide also posed severe problems for the management of the merged agency. Turf-grabbing battles broke out on the weekend in April when Reinhard and John Bernbach sent out their communications to let the managers abroad know of the deal, and some of the battles continued unresolved well into the next year. In important markets such as England and Germany, people on both sides made public statements announcing who would run the offices, trying to force the company's hand when the consolidations actually did take place. Coupled with the account losses that paralleled those in the U.S.—RJR Nabisco, for example, fired the agency internationally because it had had to resign in New York—presented headaches the Omnicom designers had never imagined.

Allen Rosenshine, Willi Schalk, and Reinhard all admit that their biggest mistake in the planning of their megamerger was not plotting the potential problems with management and personnel as carefully as they did the potential conflicts. "We have the normal but frustrating problems of ego and turf," Rosenshine says. "But this is a business built by ego and turf." The rapid progression of the merger talks, and the prospect of the Saatchi offer for DDB, drove them to announce the deal before they had had time to consider all of the ramifications.

The top executives now understand that Omnicom has affected some of its people who "suffer a sense of diminution," Rosenshine says. Even at BBDO, he admits, which has continued to prosper after the megamerger, staffers feel that their company is less prestigious because it is part of the bigger whole.

And a continuing fear about job security plagues Omnicom agencies as much as it does the entire post-megamerger ad industry. By the end of 1986, headhunters told of several thousand advertising people being out of work as a result of both mergers and cuts in client spending that spurred staff trimming in unmerged shops as well. And a November 1987 survey by *Advertising Age* showed employment down at every major shop in New York by as much as 10 percent from the beginning of 1987.

"Everything you talk about is interpreted as a job threat," Rosenshine says grimly.

He believes, and wishes that he could communicate it to the 10,000 people in his company around the world, that if the Omnicom deal had not taken place "DDB would be part of that [Saatchi & Saatchi] alphabet soup, BBDO would be fighting hostile takeovers, and Needham might not exist."

Where Omnicom and Saatchi & Saatchi have differed the most since the time of merger frenzy has been in their ability to deal with the concept of client conflicts within the holding company system. After the initial fallout of $184 million in billings from the Omnicom shops, based on the strong positions of clients such as Anheuser-Busch and General Mills Omnicom has been able to demonstrate that it truly has separate agency systems, allaying further problems arising from client mistrust. On the contrary, the win of the Discover Card account by DDB Needham Chicago late in 1987 put a second major credit card in the Omnicom system. Visa is a valued client of BBDO. And when PepsiCo wanted to move its Pizza Hut business from Chiat/Day after a few wacky years on the West Coast, it turned to its primary agency BBDO despite the McDonald's account that DDB Needham retains both internationally and on a local basis from its Washington, D.C. area office.

Saatchi & Saatchi agencies in the U.S., however, continued to be plagued by account losses due to conflicts. As talk spread through the New York rumor mills and the press about the various consolidation combinations Simonds-Gooding and his London bosses were considering just after their 1986 acquisition spree, major clients, especially Procter & Gamble, realized that they had been deceived. Just months after public statements about "autonomous networks" clients were hearing and reading on a weekly basis that their agencies were going to be merged again, and no clear plan was emerging. In order to protect themselves, the clients with the most clout went on the attack. Resign competitors within your member agencies so that we are safe when consolidations do take place, the Saatchis were told.

When Bates had to relinquish its $25 million American Cyanamid account, one of the biggest consumer-products accounts it had left, it was because of street talk regarding a Bates/Saatchi & Saatchi Compton union. P&G, a Compton client, would have found itself under the same roof with its household-products rival.

In some cases, Maurice and Charles Saatchi were successful in persuading important clients to move an account that was soon to be in a conflict situation to another agency within the Saatchi system. Such was the situation with British Airways. Saatchi's London office had won great acclaim for its "Manhattan Landing" commercial, a high-tech extravaganza that showed the island of Manhattan landing in England to make a point about how many travelers crossed the Atlantic on the British carrier. Saatchi & Saatchi Compton in New York also worked for British Airways on its stateside account. But when it finally became clear to Simonds-Gooding that he would merge DFS Dorland and Saatchi & Saatchi Compton to create a $2 billion New York office and the Saatchi & Saatchi Advertising network internationally, he had to deal with the conflict question in the airline category. DFS had recently won the merged Republic/Northwest airline in a hard-fought competition, and to give that up would have been demoralizing and costly for that agency. So British Airways quietly moved to Backer & Spielvogel for its New York business. Carl Spielvogel, all the while, denied that his agency would be merged with another in the Saatchi system, repeatedly saying to reporters, "I'm not merging with anyone."

The Saatchis also demonstrated the way they could manipulate the system in the case of the two automobile accounts that would have ended up in Saatchi & Saatchi DFS Compton when it was finally joined together in the summer of 1987. The bigger of the two car accounts was Toyota, a close to $200 million account in the DFS agency. The other half of the new giant shop worked on American Motors Corp.'s Jeep division from its Detroit office. The situation was further complicated by the pending acquisition of AMC by Chrysler Corp.

Chrysler chairman Lee Iacocca had been a constant outspoken opponent of megamergers, making one of the first speeches on the subject at the American Association of Advertising Agencies convention where Bob Jacoby was installed as chairman. Iacocca pointedly told the hundreds of agency honchos in the audience at the Greenbrier that the burden would be on them to prove the benefits that mergers would bring to clients. "What's in it for me?" He wanted to know.

But the sly Saatchis made this tricky situation work to their advantage. Since William Esty Co., the declining agency they bought in the Bates deal, had just lost its $140 million Nissan Motors account, why not try to move AMC, about $75 million, to Esty? But, they figured, let's make the client happy by keeping the same people on the account they liked when it was at Saatchi & Saatchi Compton. With the help of their new Esty chairman Joe O'Donnell, who had earned his stripes in the closeknit Detroit auto world, Saatchi management pitched the idea that they would change the name of the Detroit office of Saatchi & Saatchi Compton to William Esty, under the control of O'Donnell. The strategy worked and did much to keep Esty from going out of business after its postacquisition billings loss.

Saatchi & Saatchi moved into its consolidation phase in the second half of 1987 despite resistance from some of the agencies in question. The earnout agreement that London management had with the executives from Compton expired in 1987, and they no longer had the power to fight.

Edward L. Wax, president and chief executive officer of the New York office of Compton, much in the style of Spielvogel, put out staff memos just weeks before the announced merger denying that it would take place. Bob Levenson, the vice chairman and chief creative officer on the outs with the Saatchis since they lost Doyle Dane Bernbach to Omnicom, was pushed out of the new organization without a word.

Dancer Fitzgerald Sample emerged as the dominant New York presence in this consolidation, which is ironic in light of the Saatchis' posture when they acquired DFS a little more than a year before. That deal was not an acquisition, they insisted, they were just making a $75 million "loan" to DFS management to enable them to buy back their stock from employees and unite with Dorland to become more of an international presence. Saatchi & Saatchi would never actually own them, they said.

In July 1987, despite Spielvogel's denials of a plan that he had been part of all along, the ailing Bates agency disappeared into the conglomeration known as Backer Spielvogel Bates. Some of Bates's top people had left in advance of the deal when it became clear that there was to be no role for them in the company's future. Ralph Rydholm, for example, had been promised the vacant presidency of the New York office by Zuckert after he was reinstated by Simonds-Gooding. But Saatchi management could not put their stamp of approval on the appointment because they knew that it would not last more than several months. Rydholm, in New York for just one confounding year that had made him rich, went back to Chicago to be the top creative man at the $250 million Tatham-Laird & Kudner agency run by his friend from JWT days, Charlotte Beers.

Spielvogel's team took over at the merged agency, and all of Jacoby's cronies who had signed five-year contracts with the Saatchis were paid off and left within weeks. Zuckert, whose sense of commitment supercedes even his pride, stayed on temporarily in a nominal role, collecting his close to a million in salary, which he would still be paid when he decides to leave. "The corporate capon" is what he's been called.

Because of Backer & Spielvogel's total lack of international scope, the tenacious Larry Light found himself in a strong position after the consolidation. Light would continue as head of the international operation, which retains the Bates name, and also as the top man in his powerful post on the important Mars Inc. account.

Still more accounts, including the consumer-electronics business from Panasonic, about $25 million worth, had to be sacrificed to solve conflicts, leaving the Bates foundation even weaker and bringing about further staff cutbacks.

Having accomplished their goal of reaching the top of the heap in worldwide advertising billings, the Saatchis turned their focus to other areas. The consulting business, they had made clear years earlier, was also an important acquisition target area for the company. But when Saatchi & Saatchi unsuccessfully tried to buy two British banks in September 1987, the financial community thought they had gone a little too far. Andrew Woods, chairman of Saatchi & Saatchi Holding USA, quickly met with Wall Street analysts to explain their position. Their moves to take over Midland Bank and Hill Samuel Group, he explained, were part of the company's long-term strategy to provide financial advice to complement the company's current consulting business and to provide multinational clients with a broader range of services. In other words, Saatchi & Saatchi wanted to provide one-stop shopping for its clients.

At the end of September 1987, having reorganized the entire advertising operation of Saatchi & Saatchi, Anthony Simonds-Gooding resigned the chairmanship of the communications division to become chairman of British Satellite Broadcasting. Victor Millar, formerly of giant accounting firm Arthur Anderson & Co., took Simonds-Gooding's title, as well as continuing in his post as chairman of the company's consulting division. Simon Mellor, age thirty-two, was named deputy CEO for the communications group under Miller early in 1988.

When Saatchi & Saatchi Co. announced its earnings for the fiscal year ended September 1987, the year in which its major acquisitions were included, the results revealed the true situation. "Turnover," the U.K. equivalent of billings, were stated at $6.1 billion, showing that they never reached the $7.5 billion point the Saatchis had so broadly touted just over a year before. Pretax profits were up 77 percent, the company said, but while analysts found this figure initially impressive, they questioned whether it was really so splendid for a company that had doubled in size through acquisition.

Saatchi & Saatchi, which in December 1987 was listed for the first time on the New York Stock Exchange, bought hundreds of thousands of dollars worth of double-page ads in the *Wall Street Journal*, the *New York Times* and other major U.S. newspapers to ballyhoo these financial results. While the intention was to spark interest in its shares, the converse result, according to executives within Saatchi agencies in the U.S., was that the ads angered clients. At a time when agency compensation was a primary point of contention between advertisers and agencies, it was arrogant and unwise for the brash Britons to brag to the American financial community of their showy profitability.

The Saatchis continue to ignore protocol when it comes to boasting about their number one position. At the 1987 Paine Webber Media Outlook conference in New York one week after the fiscal 1987 earnings release, Jeremy Sinclair and Andrew Woods told hundreds of securities analysts their 1988 billings figure would be $8.3 billion. In explaining the extreme jump from the $6.1 figure announced just days before, Ann McBride, who had recently been promoted to vice chairman of the U.S. holding company division, said that figure was "annualized" to include projected new business and adjusted for new conversion rates. Of course on the chart in which this $8.3 billion figure appeared, competitors' billings were not so manipulated, making it seem as if the Saatchi lead would become even more extreme.

"Everyone knows that Bob Jacoby got enough money to compete with the Sheik of Araby," said Leonard S. Matthews, president of the A.A.A.A. at its March 1987 meeting in Boca Raton, Florida. Less than one year after Jacoby had been named to an ill-fated chairmanship of the organization, he was to be used as a symbol for the industry's problems.

"We may stand today looking more like hucksters than when

Frederic Wakeman wrote the book more than 25 years ago," Matthews said. (The book was actually published in 1946.)

The image of the advertising business, always dubious, was, indeed, damaged by the merger trend. But some ad agencies benefited a great deal.

The leaders of Young & Rubicam and Leo Burnett Co., two strong privately held agencies, took public stands on the question of mergers that set them apart from the crowd and enabled them to appear as a stable refuge for lost clients looking for a new agency home.

Alex Kroll, the chairman of the $4 billion Young & Rubicam, added $550 million in billings to the agency in 1986, much of it from megamerger fallout. Since Y&R was a privately held agency with 900 stockholders, Kroll could invest money in new services for clients without having to face securities analysts' concerns about quarterly profits and a steadily increasing stock price.

"We go to consumers for our capital; our competitors go to Wall Street for theirs," Kroll would say.

In a company memo, Kroll wrote of Y&R seeking "organic growth, in which the integrity of the company remains intact, its values and mission recognizable. . . . Advertising thrives on differentiation . . . and our competitors have handed us a wonderful difference."

In Chicago, Leo Burnett, with over $2 billion in billings, had much the same philosophy. John Kinsella, the Burnett chief executive officer who retired at the end of 1986, said the point of view of the Burnett board of directors was that public ownership was contrary to the "personal service" nature of the advertising business. "Absentee ownership in any form is inherently wrong," Kinsella said in a speech in June 1986. "You can't be semi-involved in this business. We don't want to be driven to provide quarterly earnings for outside stockholders. Cutting back on our services to make such goals is not in the best interest of our clients or employees. Nor do we want to be sidetracked by outside stockholders or security analysts. Our business is attending to clients' needs and there is precious little time to do a superior job of that as it is."

Like Young & Rubicam, Burnett was the beneficiary of new business from clients who had left the Saatchi fold, including Procter & Gamble. Burnett also became a major agency for Kraft Inc. when that Chicago marketer despaired of the disorder at JWT and looked for more stability and better service elsewhere.

The internal discontent at agencies involved in megamergers also worked to the advantage of the smaller U.S. advertising agencies, where a fertile environment for creativity was still possible. Additionally, the giant agencies found themselves closed out of almost every product category by conflicts, so agencies in the $100 to $300 million billings range were being given the opportunity to pitch for accounts of the size for which they formerly wouldn't be considered.

In the case of the $140 million Nissan Motors review, for example, it was Chiat/Day, a hot creative agency with less than $300 million in billings, that won the account after a pitch against the more marketing-oriented Tatham-Laird & Kudner, which was about the same size. Ogilvy & Mather had been in the running but had to resign to take on the Ford business that was being pulled from J. Walter Thompson.

To win the prestigious Porsche account, Minneapolis hot shop Fallon McElligott (which itself gave up part of its ownership to Scali, McCabe, Sloves for a cash infusion and a promise of independence) went against another emerging creative force, Goodby, Berlin & Silverstein, a small agency in San Francisco. Lord Geller Federico Einstein was also involved in the runoff.

Fallon McElligott bills under $175 million, but the agency's high creative profile—exemplified by its copious wins in awards competitions both in the U.S. and internationally—makes it attractive both to clients and advertising people looking for a workplace that will constructively build their careers.

Hal Riney, the brilliant advertising writer who brought the world such diverse creations as the adventures of Bartles & Jaymes and the romantic Italian weddings of Gallo wine commercials, was one of the early symbols of the virtues of the midsize independent shop. Just before merger mania erupted, Riney, who headed Ogilvy & Mather's San Francisco office, wanted to spin off on his own, partly because his branch was blocked by conflicts with O&M clients and could not grow. His agency, which grew to have offices in Chicago and New York, offers an environment for the ad person who is interested in making good advertising, in contrast with being part of a profit-crazed conglomerate.

Other midsize and small shops such as Hill Holliday Connors Cosmopulous, Boston, known for its sensitive John Hancock Financial Services "Real Life, Real Answers" campaigns, and Levine, Huntley, Schmidt & Beaver, the New York agency that created the zany Subaru spots, began to figure prominently in account pitches and awards shows in the post-megamerger scene.

As 1987 came to a close, the publicly held advertising agencies, despite staff cuts and cost controls that boosted profits, saw their stock prices drop by as much as 40 to 50 percent when the stock market crashed. Allen Rosenshine said the primary effect on the agencies would be to curtail further deal making on the part of the publicly held shops.

The shrinking stock prices may, however, provide bargains for those adland emperors who still want to fight their way back into the picture. Bob Jacoby, following the settlement of his arbitration with the Saatchis, which netted him another $4.7 million and will free him from his no-compete clause in September 1988, already has made some moves in that direction. Jacoby and John Hoyne bought a significant amount of stock in the prestigious Ogilvy & Mather agency, and Hoyne encouraged rumors that he wanted to take over the company. The two sold their shares at a tremendous profit after driving up the stock several points, when O&M management made clear that they would fight such a takeover.

Jacoby also has privately voiced his desire to buy a consumer-products company "so that I could sit on the other side of the table and tell the agency how to write copy."

Few industry observers doubt that Jacoby, who likes to brag that he can earn $20,000 interest each day on the money he made from the Saatchis, will resurface in the advertising business. He and his pal Hoyne meet often in Manhattan and cook up schemes over an afternoon of lunch and cocktails. Hoyne looked at agencies ranging from Tatham-Laird & Kudner to Wells, Rich, Greene to Jordan Case Taylor & McGrath, plotting various combinations if he were to succeed in buying one or all of the privately held shops.

And as Bob Jacoby told the *New York Times*: "It would be fun to have something that would get me closer to knocking off the Saatchis. It's easy to do because I can see these guys are amateurs."

NOTES

$\mathbf{T}$he primary source for the information contained in this book is scores of interviews with the people involved in the story.

The executives with first-hand knowledge of the events shared their experiences and points of view, with the exception of the management of Saatchi & Saatchi Co. Despite numerous requests, Maurice and Charles Saatchi declined to be interviewed. Simon Mellor, who at the time of the interview for this book was corporate development director at the company, was the only executive made available.

Other information, in the form of press releases, media reports, and interviews with sources inside the companies was accumulated in the course of my daily reporting on the events described in the book and many follow-up interviews. I was present at many of the meetings and conventions depicted, so the impressions and recreations are from first-hand knowledge.

I also had access to the normal financial reports of the publicly held companies, and many of the financial and legal documents filed with the Securities and Exchange Commission regarding the merger and acquisition deals discussed in the book.

The clips from the authoritative *Advertising Age* library were important in compiling information from the years before 1976, when I began my own reporting on the field. Clips from other publications including *Business Week*, the *Wall Street Journal*, *Fortune*, the *New York Times* and *Adweek*, as well as the British magazines *Business* and *Campaign*, helped to form my files on the companies described here.

Three books also contributed some information. Russ Johnson's *Marion Harper: An Unauthorized Biography* (Crain Books, 1982) was key in describing the end of Harper's control over Interpublic.

Robert Levenson's *Bill Bernbach's Book*, (Villard Books, 1987) also provided information about Doyle Dane Bernbach.

The Saatchi & Saatchi Story by Philip Kleinman (Weidenfeld & Nicolson, 1987) was also a background source.

The following citations identify all quotations that were not from my own reporting. Credit also is given here to the original sources of facts that came from press reports.

CHAPTER 2

"Talk about guys who had no outside interests," says Don Zuckert, who worked for him. "His big joy on weekends was to go home and write memos—nasty memos." New York Times, October 5, 1986.

"Privately held," Jacoby said, "Bates would be tenth next year and 15th the year after." *Fortune*, June 23, 1986.

CHAPTER 3

"Saatchi has an absolutely unbounded, avaricious desire to be the biggest in everything they do," according to Ron Leagas, a former managing director of the agency in London. "They don't see why they should be second best at anything." *Advertising Age*, May 22, 1986.

[The Saatchis] were "immature as businessmen," when they began in 1970, "but extremely dynamic and terrific opportunists," says Ron Legas. *Business*, May, 1986.

CHAPTER 4
"Despite their dynamic fronts, a lot of agencies are pretty laissez-faire organizations. Whenever Saatchi read in the press that a client was reviewing his account, the first reaction was: 'Right, who knows him? Get on the phone now.' The second response was to kick the new business director in the balls for not getting us on the shortlist beforehand." *Business*, May, 1986.

In 1979, another agency chief in London, the flamboyant Peter Marsh of Allen Brady & Marsh, was quoted as saying, "A year ago I had lunch with Maurice Saatchi. He told me that before too long Saatchi & Saatchi Garland Compton would be the biggest agency in Britain, that we would be No. 2, and that no one had yet woke up to it." *Advertising Age*, August 20, 1979.

CHAPTER 5
John O'Toole's account of his breakfast with Maurice Saatchi. *Advertising Age*, May 12, 1986.

"P&G is generally credited with having decided long ago that competition between brands was inevitable, and that no brand —not even the most impressive—could garner more than a share of any market. Therefore, said P&G, if we must split the market with other brands, why should they not be our own brands instead of some other company's?" *Advertising Age*, October 21, 1963.

CHAPTER 6
"We seem to have been able to put together a microcosm of the General Motors pattern, where there are competitive divisions responsible to a central office, and if it does anything, it will

probably increase or enhance competition among the various agency segments that make up Interpublic," Adams said. *Advertising Age*, June 5, 1972.

"We are not what you'd call bosom buddies," Spielvogel said.

"We're not 24. We come out of the world's largest ad complex and together stand unchallenged as the world's smallest agency."

"We're looking for the kind of client that knows the difference between good advertising and froth," Backer said.

"We're not interested in outside investors and won't ever go public." (Spielvogel) *Advertising Age*, June 25, 1979.

"And we want to remain private," Spielvogel stressed, noting the equity share by only the six original partners. "Nothing is for sale here except our services," he insisted. *Advertising Age*, May 19, 1980.

CHAPTER 8

"If we are to advance," Bernbach wrote, "we must emerge as a distinctive personality. We must develop our own philosophy and not have the advertising philosophy of others imposed on us.

"Let us blaze new trails. Let us prove to the world that good taste, good art, good writing can be good selling." *Bill Bernbach's Book* by Robert Levenson.

CHAPTER 9

Luisi said her case would be based on the combination of pressure from management for "big projections and a total lack of financial controls," at the company that made management responsible for creating "a breeding ground" from which the barter syndication scandal arose. *Advertising Age*, April 18, 1983.

CHAPTER 10

As Kenneth Roman, president of the Ogilvy Group said when he heard the news from Dougherty of the Times, "That takes the game to a new level." *New York Times*, April 18, 1986.

CHAPTER 11

Spielvogel said at the time he was afraid his agency's lack of international resources would lead to the loss of major accounts. He explained that when his client Philip Morris Cos. took over General Foods, people at his agency were "rubbing their hands with glee" at the "long-term opportunity to go to work for General Foods." But, he said, his competitors, the "900-lb. gorillas," giant agencies like Young & Rubicam and Ogilvy & Mather . . . *Advertising Age*, April 21, 1986.

CHAPTER 13

Executives of major package goods marketers were quoted in the press as saying the megamerger tend made them feel slighted. "The client is an after thought and is getting lost in the shuffle. We want an agency who really wants our business, who would kill to get our business." *Advertising Age*, June 2, 1986.

Interview with Robert Goldstein of Procter & Gamble on megamergers. *Advertising Age*, June 2, 1986.

CHAPTER 14

"Clearly we must be the major new business target of every agency in town," Zuckert told the New York Times. "On the one hand they're saying this is bad for the industry, and then they're giving all these stories to the press about how awful megamergers are. I wish Ed Ney [Young & Rubicam chairman] would put us in Y&R's profit sharing plan. We've given them half of their new business this year." *New York Times*, October 5.

"What's changed is that [Saatchi seems] to be leading with their chin, to be providing evidence that their critics have been right all along," said James Dougherty, vice president of research at County Securities. *Advertising Age*, September 29, 1986.

CHAPTER 15
[O'Donnell] was disturbed by the practice of paying employees in the company's office in Belgium partly by expense vouchers to help them avoid local taxes. He also found that part of the sum paid to the owners of an ad agency in Turkey purchased by JWT in 1974 was deposited in a Swiss bank account, allegedly to help the owners to avoid local taxes. *Wall Street Journal*, June 17, 1987.

CHAPTER 16
Over breakfast in the London banking firm's private dining room, the team planned how the little minnow from London could devour the bloated American fish. *New York Times*, July 9, 1987.

CHAPTER 17
"It would be fun to have something that would get me closer to knocking off the Saatchis," Jacoby says. "It's easy to do because I can see these guys are amateurs." *New York Times Magazine*, November 8, 1987.

APPENDICES

Omnicom Group

BBDO Worldwide

Diversified Agency Services

Tracy-Locke/Cargill Wilson & Acree
Blair Advertising
CAK
Kressen Craig/D.I.K.
Doremus & Co.
Doremus Porter Novelli
Rapp & Collins USA
Kallir, Philips Ross
York Alpern
HMC
RC Communications
Promotion Dynamics
Weiss/Watson
Bernard Hodes
GM Dubois
Franklin Spier
Maltese

DDB Needham Worldwide

SOURCE: Omnicom Group

Saatchi & Saatchi Co. PLC

Consulting

YSW/Clancy Shulman
Gamma
Hay Group
Cleveland Consulting
McBen
Litigation Sciences
Peterson
MSL International
Moxon Dolphin & Kerby

Communications

SAATCHI & SAATCHI ADVERTISING WORLDWIDE	BACKER SPIELVOGEL BATES WORLDWIDE	SAATCHI & SAATCHI ADVERTISING AFFILIATES USA	SAATCHI & SAATCHI MARKETING SERVICES USA	SAATCHI & SAATCHI ADVERTISING AFFILIATES AND MARKETING SERVICES (INTL)
• Saatchi & Saatchi DFS America • Saatchi & Saatchi Advertising Intl	• Backer & Spielvogel/Bates (USA) and Ted Bates International • Kobs & Brady Direct Marketing Worldwide • Dorlands	• William Esty (including Detroit) • Campbell-Mithun (Minneapolis/Chicago) • AC&R/Diener Hauser Bates & Bess • Rumrill-Hoyt (Rochester) • Klemtner • Conill • McCaffrey & McCall (including Rumrill-Hoyt [NY]) • Cochrane Chase Livingston	• Howard Marlboro • Siegel & Gale • Rowland Company (PR) • CMS • Kleid • BTD	• Sallingbury Casey • Grandfield Rork Collins Financial Ltd • Halls of Scotland • KMP Humphreys Bull & Barker Ltd • Harrison Cowley • RPG • ICM International Ltd • Rowland Co. Worldwide • Siegel & Gale Intl

SOURCE: Saatchi & Saatchi Co. January 1988

APPENDICES

Principals in the Emperors of Adland story

Neil Austrian—Former chief executive officer of Doyle Dane Bernbach

William Backer—co-founder of Backer & Spielvogel, now president of Backer Speilvogel Bates

Charlotte Beers—chairman of Tatham-Laird & Kudner

John L. Bernbach—son of William Bernbach, now president and chief operating officer of DDB Needham Worldwide

William Bernbach—the late founder of Doyle Dane Bernbach

Norman W. Brown—chairman and chief executive officer of Foote, Cone & Belding Communications

Eileen Drgon—former secretary to Ted Bates Worldwide chairman Robert Jacoby

Philip B. Dusenberry—chairman and chief creative officer of BBDO Worldwide (a division of Omnicom Group)

Philip H. Geier Jr.—chairman, president and chief executive officer of Interpublic Group of Cos.

Robert Goldstein—the late vice president of advertising, Procter & Gamble, killed in a rafting accident, August, 1987

Marion Harper—founder of Interpublic Group of Cos.

John Hoyne—former president of Ted Bates Worldwide's international division

Robert Jacoby—former chairman Ted Bates Worldwide

Don Johnston—former chairman JWT Group

Robert Levenson—former vice chairman Doyle Dane Bernbach and Saatchi & Saatchi Compton, now at Scali, McCabe, Sloves

Barry Loughrane—former chairman and chief executive officer Doyle Dane Bernbach, now chairman and chief executive officer Diversified Agency Services

Marie Luisi—former senior vice president and head of the syndication unit of J. Walter Thompson Co.

Burton J. Manning—chairman of J. Walter Thompson Co. (division of WPP Group)

Simon Mellor—deputy chairman of Saatchi & Saatchi Communications

John H. Nichols—former executive vice president, Ted Bates Worldwide

Walter J. O'Brien—former vice chairman of J. Walter Thompson Co., now chief executive officer O'Rielly O'Brien Clow/RSCG

Joseph W. O'Donnell—former chairman and chief executive officer J. Walter Thompson Co., now chairman and chief executive officer of William Esty Co., division of Saatchi & Saatchi Co.

John O'Toole—former chairman of Foote, Cone & Belding Communications, now executive vice president, American Association of Advertising Agencies

John E. Peters—former president and chief operating officer of J. Walter Thompson Co., now associated with WPP Group

Keith Reinhard—chairman and chief executive officer of DDB Needham Worldwide, division of Omnicom Group

Allen Rosenshine—president and chief executive officer, Omnicom Group

Ralph Rydholm—former executive vice president at J. Walter Thompson Co. and Ted Bates Worldwide, now managing partner at Tatham-Laird & Kudner

Charles Saatchi—co-founder of Saatchi & Saatchi Co.

Maurice Saatchi—co-founder and chairman of Saatchi & Saatchi Co.

Willi Schalk—president and chief operating officer of BBDO Worldwide, division of Omnicom Group.

Anthony Simonds-Gooding—former chairman of Saatchi & Saatchi Communications

Martin Sorrell—former financial director of Saatchi & Saatchi Co., now chairman of WPP Group

Carl Spielvogel—chairman of Backer Spielvogel Bates

Jennifer Van Liew—former secretary and then international coordinator at Ted Bates Worldwide

Andrew Woods—chairman of Saatchi & Saatchi USA Holdings

Donald Zuckert—former chairman of Ted Bates Worldwide, now president of Backer Spielvogel Bates